Child Support and
Public Policy

Child Support and Public Policy

Securing Support from Absent Fathers

Judith Cassetty
The University of Texas

Lexington Books
D.C. Heath and Company
Lexington, Massachusetts
Toronto

Library of Congress Cataloging in Publication Data

Cassetty, Judith.
   Child support and public policy.

   Bibliography: p.
   Includes index.
   1. Support (Domestic relations)—United States. 2. Father-separated children. I. Title.
HV741.C337   362.7'1   77-4541
ISBN 0-669-01486-9

Published simultaneously in Canada.

Printed in the United States of America.

International Standard Book Number: 0-669-01486-9

Library of Congress Catalog Card Number: 77-4541

To Perian and Elliott

Contents

List of Tables

Preface

Professional and public concern with the rapidly rising incidence of family dissolution, illegitimacy, and the increasing representation of female-headed families among the ranks of the poor, has focused awareness on the struggle that these female-headed families face in maintaining themselves. Dialogue addressing these essentially economic problems has resulted in proposals for a variety of social welfare policy strategies. Many of these strategies—such as the provision of educational and vocational services to female heads of families and daycare for their children—emphasize the importance of helping these women to compensate for the social handicap of not having a male earner in the family. Other strategies, such as providing a "children's allowance" or subsidized wages for persons with low earning ability, (relative to the number of their dependents), focus on society's responsibility to insure that its least powerful members—its children—enjoy equal opportunity to reach their full potential.

Although there may be some disagreement regarding the degree of emphasis to be placed on each of the previously-stated strategies, few would question the worthiness of the goal. Problems often arise, however, when enforcement of the parental child support obligation is introduced as a strategy for helping single, divorced, or separated women to maintain homes for their children. Individuals whose attitudes place them at all points on the political spectrum fear that further public involvement in child support enforcement is tantamount to greater intrusion by government into the private lives of families, thus, eroding further the freedoms of self-determination and privacy. Others are concerned that public policy which fosters enforcement of the parental support obligation is a shabby cloak to disguise the reluctance of some members of society to accept economic responsibility for other, less able members. Both of these views imply a perception of public policy as similar to falling dominoes—almost impossible to check once begun, and total in its consequences. I do not believe either of these to be necessarily the end result of such "intrusion." Public policy can modify social institutions—alter them without destroying their basic fabric. In order to modify and improve these institutions, however, it is imperative to know where we *are,* where we *want to be,* and the costs, (both real and personal), of arriving at our goal.

For this reason we must recognize that fears such as those stated earlier are *not* frivolous or ill-founded, though they may be overstated in terms of their ultimate consequences. *Some* erosion of the personal freedom of *some* adults may, in fact, be part of the costs of insuring equitable treatment, vis-à-vis child support enforcement, for *other* adults and their children. How high the price we are willing to pay to achieve any given end is a political question. What prices are associated with what alternative ends is an empirical question. It is the business of policy research to formulate and address empirical questions, and it is within the policy-making sphere that choices are made and courses of action are charted. One set of pursuits—research or action—is never totally independent of the other, whether the topic is energy policy or child support enforcement policy. However, because the boundaries of what we might call "child support enforcement policy" have not yet been defined, the confusion between the political questions and the empirical questions is likely to be more pronounced than it is in other policy areas. The reader will be cautioned against making this error, although it is possible that the author herself has unwittingly committed it on occasion.

A second note of caution, which relates closely to the first, regards the strength and direction of our findings and, consequently, the strength of our policy recommendations. Chapters 3, 4, and 5 represent original attempts to explore aspects of the child support phenomenon that had never before been examined in such ways. The results, therefore, should be viewed as highly tentative, and in need of much more exploration. The value of this publication lies in the new perspective on the child support enforcement issue which I hope to impart to the reader. It is my fondest wish that many, many more questions—empirical *and* political arise as a consequence of those I have addressed in these pages.

Finally, though I have chosen to focus my analyses and discussion on the issue of child support enforcement policy as it relates to the female-headed family and the absent father, this choice in no way reflects a normative stance. The reader should understand from the outset that this author favors child support enforcement policy which insures equal treatment of *both* parents, regardless of the sex of the custodial parent, and focus on the *female*-headed family serves a purely pragmatic function.

Acknowledgments

The author gratefully acknowledges the receipt of support for her research from the Institute for Research on Poverty at the University of Wisconsin, Madison, Wisconsin, and the Center for Social Work Research at the University of Texas at Austin. Some of the data utilized in this book were made available by the Inter-University Consortium for Political and Social Research. The data were originally collected by the Survey Research Center, University of Michigan at Ann Arbor, and analyzed under sponsorship of the Institute for Research on Poverty and the Center for Social Work Research. Neither the original source or collectors of the data, nor the Consortium or sponsors of the research reported herein, bear any responsibility for the analyses or interpretations. These are the sole responsibility of the author.

Though ultimate responsibility rests with the author, a number of persons have made substantial contributions toward the beginning which this volume represents. Lacking an ample body of scientific literature that addresses the topic of child support, the author was forced to rely initially upon her personal experience and the experience of countless other women, men, and children who are involved in one way or another with the child support system. To these persons, known and unknown, is due the greatest debt.

Second, the author is deeply indebted to Irwin Garfinkel at the University of Wisconsin, who supervised and helped guide the doctoral dissertation that formed the core of this book. Others who read and lent substantive criticism to drafts at various stages of development include Robert Lampman, Al Kadushin, Joseph Heffernan, and Rodney Erickson.

Expert technical assistance, primarily in the form of the construction of a data file at the Institute for Research on Poverty and the University of Wisconsin, was provided by Louise Cunliffe and Nancy Williamson, whose help was virtually indispensable during the early months of the project. Mary Hall and Ed Naylor, the latter under sponsorship of the Center for Social Work Research at the University of Texas, provided most of the computer programming expertise over a period exceeding two years. Without the skill and attention to detail that these four persons brought to this project, it would have languished long ago.

Finally, the patience of Job was necessary in order that the typing of the many, many drafts of this manuscript in its various developmental stages was ever accomplished. Those numerous individuals who formed the typists' pools at both the Institute for Research on Poverty and the School of Social Work at the University of Texas contributed anonymously to the effort, but are not unappreciated. Mary Tittel, Joan Ward, Susan Matoska, and Rita Soto made substantial typing and editorial contributions to the final manuscript.

There are undoubtedly many others whose comments and efforts have been incorporated at some point during the study. Only space and time prevent explicit acknowledgment of their indispensable aid.

Part I
Child Support and the Dependent Family: The System Today

1

The Status of Child Support Enforcement in America Today

Introduction

The topic of child support—that is, the money which men pay to women who have custody of the children who were products of their union—has not been a topic of general concern until rather recently. Although we recognize, and will later document, that men have taken and been granted custody of their children following marital dissolution with greater frequency in recent years, their numbers are still quite small compared with those of women who have custody or conservatorship of their children. Therefore, we will continue to focus on female heads of families, although we recognize the existence of exceptions to this post-split custom and take the position that child support policy should apply equally in both instances. Prior to the 1960s, when feminists began expressing their concern with the inadequacy of the legal system for purposes of securing and enforcing the child support obligation, the public attitude which prevailed was that economic support of nonpoor children was usually a private matter to be decided by the two adult parties involved and, when disputed, resolved within the judicial arena at private—not public—cost. Absent fathers complained that their payments were too high and mothers with custody of minor children complained that child support payments were too low and an unreliable source of income. Public concern with the issue of child support enforcement was limited to a small number of welfare administrators and politicians who perceived it exclusively in terms of its potential for reducing the economic costs of public dependence.

In spite of this limited but certainly not trivial concern, there have been few efforts to examine the child support enforcement system for the purpose of responding to these charges, and no efforts which could be considered thorough.

Academic inquiry into the nature and boundaries of the system of child support enforcement in this country has been limited to a bare handful of articles and empirical studies by social scientists. The literature generated by those in the legal or judicial profession, though somewhat more abundant than that from other disciplines, has been concerned primarily with issues that have direct impact upon the practice of law by those attorneys who specialize in family law, and who practice principally in the private sector. Much of this discussion has centered around the implications for the practice of family law brought about by changes in the Family Code or its interpretation, issues involving rules of evidence and procedure for establishing, enforcing, and modifying the support obligation, and problems related to the collection of legal fees.[1]

Within other social-science disciplines, notably sociology, economics, and social work, the dearth of quantitative information as to the impact and boundaries of the child support enforcement system is astounding in light of the enormous number of persons who are presumably affected in ways that traditionally have been of concern to social scientists in those disciplines. With few exceptions,[2] the literature from these and other social-science disciplines has largely ignored the child support phenomenon.

As a consequence of this neglect, we are abysmally ignorant of the facts pertaining to the scope, dynamics, and impact of the child support system in America today.

In spite of limited knowledge, there have been several efforts to reform the system in recent years. However, these efforts have been based largely upon the perceptions of policymakers as to where the flaws in the system lie, and not upon systematic data-based examination. As a consequence, reform has been piecemeal and perhaps inadequate. As we shall later see, much of the impetus for these attempts at reform has come from the public, not the private, sector. It is primarily when the private system of establishing and enforcing the child support obligation fails and a custodial mother finds herself with insufficient resources for self-support that public concern with enforcing the support obligation manifests itself.

In other words, the efforts that have been made to place child support enforcement among the functions of government have been directed largely at the poor and closely associated with concern for protection of the public purse.

The present system for enforcing the parental child support obligation—an obligation mandated by the civil code in every state—is such that a woman who is economically able to do so may purchase the services of an attorney to pursue a support award, or its enforcement or modification, through the legal maze. If she is unable to purchase these services in the private marketplace, many communities provide a limited enforcement service, usually on a sliding-fee basis. The limitations on the services provided (e.g., there must be a standing court order for support with which the obligor has been out of compliance for a period of time), together with lengthy waiting periods which result from the excessive demand for these services, discourage many women and social agencies from using this process. In addition, few of these local programs have the legal authority to initiate action against the absent parent. Thus, the custodial parent has the sole responsibility for taking legal action against the noncompliant parent. The time and energy required to initiate and follow through on such suits (often repeatedly) discourage many women from pursuing support from a recalcitrant parent.

It is often difficult to justify the expenditure of public moneys on child support enforcement, since social benefits are difficult to measure and limited-income female heads of families do not represent a strong political constituency whose votes must be cultivated. In the event a female head of a family including children finds herself requesting Aid to Families with Dependent Children (AFDC)—far too often the case—she will have cost-free legal services for the purpose of securing and enforcing the child support obligation. Indeed, as we shall later see, she has little choice in the matter, for she is compelled to cooperate fully in the identification, location, and enforcement activity lest she be excluded by federal law from AFDC benefits.

The overall picture, then, is that the child support enforcement system in America today is a fractured one which subjects members of different socioeconomic classes to different institutional constraints. By itself, this is cause for concern. In addition, if this differential treatment results in disparity in the frequency with which child support is received and in the levels of payments, there is even greater cause for concern.

Whether or not this public-private mix—this dual system of enforcement of the child support obligation—is functional, equitable, and efficient is but one set of questions to be answered. Prior to making public choices based upon the answer to those questions, however, it is necessary to explore a number of components of the system in order to gain some preliminary understanding of its overall impact.

At the very least, we need to answer the following specific questions: What are the demographic characteristics of the child support-dependent population and of the parents who do not live in the same household with their children? Which of these characteristics are associated with more frequent and higher levels of child support? Is the present status of child support consistent with expectations as to absent fathers' ability to pay? Are publicly supported child support enforcement programs likely to be cost-effective? It is only after these questions are answered that we will be in a position to begin a discussion of whether or not reform of the system appears warranted, and in what direction.

We will continue our present chapter with a history of familial responsibility for the economic welfare of kin as reflected in the development of publicly supported transfer programs, including the development of the state programs designed to identify and locate absent fathers for the purpose of securing support from them for their dependent children, and the federalization of these programs. In conclusion we will identify empirical questions and specify which of these will be addressed in later chapters.

The History and Tradition of Public Child Support Enforcement Policy

We can trace the "relatives' responsibility" tradition within our public assistance programs back to 1597, in Section 7, Chapter 3, 39th Elizabeth, an Act for the Relief of the Poor, which states:

That the parents or children of every poor, old, blind, lame and impotent person, or other poor person not able to work, being of sufficient ability, shall at their own charges relieve and maintain every such poor person in that manner and according to that rate as by the justices at their general quarter session shall be assessed.[3]

This charge—to insure the economic support of one's parents or children—was to remain intact for more than three hundred years in both welfare statutes and civil codes in England and in the United States.

The gradual erosion of the requirement that adult children take responsibility for their aged or infirm indigent parents began in this country with the failure of some newer states, principally those in the South and West, to enact filial responsibility laws as had those in the East, which had been influenced more by the Puritan traditions. It has been suggested by Alvin Schorr that enforcement of filial responsibility eroded more quickly in this country than did enforcement of parental responsibility because of the fact that aged parents continued to maintain ownership of their farmlands until death, when their children, who had been living with their elderly parents, became owners. The elderly were thus not economically dependent until after the rise of industrialized cities, which broke this centuries-old tradition by luring the young from their parents' rural homes. The elderly parents were then left without kin to work the farms when they became too feeble to do so, and the children grew old in the cities where few had maintained the tradition of living in extended family arrangements. Separate homesites and growing geographic separation owing to the westward movement tended to erode filial ties. Schorr points out that the timing and geographic location of renewed attempts at enforcement of filial responsibility laws corresponded with sharp rises in the numbers of indigent aged.[4]

The traditions of filial responsibility which had been enunciated in the Poor Laws were incorporated in early Social Security legislation, which provided for survivors' benefits to be paid to the aged, dependent parents of a covered wage earner in the event of his or her death. The public assistance portion of the Social Security Act, which set up the adult categories including Old Age Assistance, left the question of filial responsibility up to the states. By 1952, most of the states had legislation requiring support that was clearly applicable to OAA recipients only, seven states had general legislation that did not specifically apply to OAA recipients, and twelve had no legislation at all which required support.[5] The last vestiges of economic responsibility for aged or disabled parents was removed from their adult children by the time OAA was federalized in 1973. No longer are the children of SSI recipients subjected to a means test. This decline in public assistance regulations that were designed to foster filial responsibility has corresponded with a diminution in the proportion of the elderly who had been employed in "uncovered" occupations, as well as a decline in the proportion of the poor who were aged.[6]

As more elderly people became eligible for Social Security benefits, fewer were to be found in poverty. Thus, there has been less necessity for enforcing filial responsibility as a means of limiting public assistance expenditures.

The responsibility of parents for the economic maintenance of their minor children has not been eroded as has that of adults for their aged parents. In fact, as we shall see later, there has been a trend in recent years to accelerate the enforcement of the parental support obligation.

As with laws requiring adult children to support their aged parents, the public is not concerned with the enforcement of child support unless the dependent person is poor. Even in states whose civil codes allow it, it is unlikely that parents with incomes lower than public assistance standards can compel support from a wealthy child, no matter how desperate their circumstances. The occasional public enforcement of filial support laws has only been stimulated in times of sharply rising public assistance costs.[7] Similarly, concern with the public enforcement of child support has grown stronger as the AFDC-recipient population (and concomitant costs) has risen with increases in the number of poor, female-headed households.

In 1950, because of congressional concern that greater efforts should be made to enforce the assumption of parental responsibility in families receiving what was then called ADC, the NOLEO ("notice to law enforcement officials") amendment was added to Title IV D of the Social Security Act. In order to continue to receive federal moneys for state-administered welfare programs, the states were required to "provide prompt notice to appropriate law-enforcement officials, of the furnishing of aid to dependent children in respect of a child who has been deserted or abandoned by a parent."[8]

This represented the first time since the passage of the Social Security Act that states were *mandated* to involve themselves in the legal process for enforcing a civil code. In addition, NOLEO marked the point at which the option for taking legal action against the father of her child was removed from a woman applying for or receiving public aid. "In this way the public welfare agency, in addition to being the instrument of providing financial assistance and services for rehabilitation, became a vehicle of social compulsion."[9] Although the author is cognizant of the fact that the public welfare system has, both before and after the passage of NOLEO, intruded on the private lives of recipients in a similar fashion in other ways, it is my purpose herein to confine my remarks to the relationship between a mother and the father(s) of her child(ren) in regard to the issue of economic support and eligibility for public assistance.

In an effort to facilitate enforcement of NOLEO, the Uniform Reciprocal Enforcement of Support Act (URESA) was promulgated by the National Conference on Uniform State Laws in 1950. Within a short time, all the states, plus the District of Columbia, Guam, Puerto Rico, and the Virgin Islands (and, very recently, Canada), had made formal agreements with one another and/or enacted legislation consistent with URESA. The specific provisions preclude the possibility that movement across state lines per se will facilitate the avoidance of the obligation of a parent to support his children. Thus, the parent with custody does not have to go to the errant parent's state of residence to secure support through his court of jurisdiction, nor does the absent parent have to be extradited to the state in which the dependent children live.[10] It was felt by policymakers that the adoption of URESA by all of the states, together with the NOLEO welfare amendment of 1950, would facilitate the enforcement of support for AFDC-dependent children and thus help reduce the public outlay for this group. Over the years, the Conference on Uniform State Laws has continued to revise URESA, tightening loopholes where they might appear, in attempts to improve its effectiveness.

That the intrusion into the previously private decisions of families should have come about in the form of the NOLEO amendment is not surprising in light of what had been happening to the AFDC population. Liberalized welfare regulations in the forties had shortened waiting periods for establishment of "continued absence" of the father from the home and lifted restrictions that had previously excluded illegitimate children from eligibility. These, together with the increasing rates of divorce, separation, and illegitimacy, have resulted in an unexpected burgeoning of the welfare rolls.[11]

The inherent policy conflict—between the public commitment to meet the basic economic needs of children and the policy of enforcing the assumption of responsibility by fathers—has persisted through the years. Each round of increasingly liberalized welfare eligibility requirements has been followed by increases in the number of recipients, which have in turn been followed by attempts to "stem the welfare tide." All the while, the pool of potential welfare recipients has been expanding due to increased rates of marital disruption and illegitimacy. Various attempts have been made to reduce the demand for AFDC by tightening up welfare regulations, producing dubious results,[12] and leaving but one principle avenue for reducing the public burden: shift the burden back onto the family itself. This can be accomplished in one of three ways. First, the parents, both mothers and fathers, can be required to take more economic responsibility for their children (e.g., employment or WIN requirements for mothers as conditions for AFDC eligibility, and child support enforcement through wage garnishment and other efforts focused upon the absent fathers). Second, severe benefit limits can be imposed. Finally, application for AFDC can be made so difficult or embarrassing that women choose to get along however they can without it. All avenues can, of course, be pursued simultaneously, though the latter requires an enormous amount of administrative skill to insure that the distasteful aspects of the application and recertification process are not so blatantly discriminatory as to be readily overturned as a consequence of legal protest.

The combined success of NOLEO and URESA, in terms of reducing the demand or need for AFDC by facilitating support by the absent father, cannot be accurately assessed. Annual caseloads, as well as recipient rates, continued to climb.[13] Between January 1952 and December 1954, according to a study by the U.S. Bureau of Public Assistance, the number of AFDC applicants who withdrew their applications rather than agree to have the Notice to Law Enforcement Officials sent declined from 7.9 to 4.2 percent.[14] It appears then, that there was some discouraging, or "rationing," effect, though its strength declined over time. It is likely that some of these applicants learned how to circumvent the policy or went elsewhere to apply for assistance. It is also likely that word got around, and other applicants did not have to learn by their own experience how to be granted assistance without having to initiate legal action against the fathers of their children. Another possibility is that over time fewer and fewer women objected to the requirement.

What is also likely is that conscious or unconscious collusion between welfare department personnel and their clients must have occurred. Many social workers were of the opinion that forcing clients to take legal action against the absent parent only impeded, if not prevented, reconciliation, a primary goal of casework services directed at these clients.[15] As client autonomy and self-determination have traditionally been highly valued by social workers, welfare caseworkers were, as a group, probably inclined to neglect enforcing this regulation when clients were not interested in the pursuit of support from the absent parent, or when it seemed contrary to the best interests of the dependent family.

By 1967, Congress was apparently convinced that the NOLEO requirement and the supporting legislation, URESA, were not effective enough in terms of reducing the growing AFDC costs and caseloads, for the Senate Finance Committee instituted what it believed would be an effective program of enforcement of child support and determination of paternity. It proposed Social Security amendments requiring that the state welfare agency establish a single, identified unit, whose purpose was to undertake to establish paternity of each child receiving welfare who was born out of wedlock and to secure support for him or her.[16] This proposed legislation was adopted, and the scope of involvement in the legal and domestic affairs of the poor was thus broadened. The state now had mandate not only to notify law enforcement officials that the civil code requiring fathers to provide support was being violated, but also to initiate and accomplish the activity of determining paternity.

The results of the legislation were mixed. In spite of the fact that the federal government was to provide 50 percent matching funds for increased efforts in child support enforcement, by 1971 only 13.4 percent of absent parents of AFDC-dependent children paid child support (though in what amounts was not reported), and a General Accounting Office report in 1972 stated that 34 percent of the absent parents in three states surveyed had not even been located. According to those within the federal government who advocated child support and paternity reform, the primary obstacles to increased cost-effectiveness were legal and administrative. The courts had held, for instance, that the Social Security Act as written did not allow the states to require that a mother cooperate in locating an absent parent as a condition of eligibility. Although some states, notably California, had found legal bases for circumventing the prohibition, these were deemed "less secure than a Federal statutory provision would be."[17]

Another obstacle to reform, critical in the view of many, was restrictions on the use of certain potential sources of information as to the whereabouts of absent parents. The testimony of the U.S. senator from Georgia, Sam Nunn, before the U.S. Senate Committee on Finance in September 1973 was typical: ". . . A parent locator service would (should) be established within the Department of Justice to gather information as to the location of absent parents. Access to *all Federal and participating State records* would assist in location."[18] Most others at the hearings were of like mind, and most remaining issues to be resolved had to do with the type of administrative structure such a new program would take, the nature of the incentives for participation by state and local welfare departments as well as incentives for the AFDC applicant to cooperate, and sanctions against the absent parent for noncompliance.

The culmination of this incremental process in a federal child support enforcement program is not illogical, nor is it particularly surprising that there has been no substantial objection voiced by welfare applicants and recipients or social workers and AFDC program administrators, for there is general agreement that the paternal support obligation is a fundamental one. What is surprising, however, is that a program so extensive and costly was launched with so little concrete evidence as to its ultimate economic value.

The congressional decision to initiate this program most likely was more political than economic. From the time of the initial formal hearings in September 1973 until Public Law 93-647, Part B of Title XX, was passed during the Christmas adjournment rush of 1974,[19] hearings were simultaneously being conducted on what was to become Part A of the same Social Security Amendments Act of 1974.

Part A of the Social Security Amendments Act authorized appropriations for the following social-services purposes:

(1) Achieving or maintaining economic self-support to prevent, reduce, or eliminate dependency;
(2) Achieving or maintaining self-sufficiency, including reduction or prevention of dependency;
(3) Preventing or remedying neglect, abuse, or exploitation of children and adults unable to protect their own interests, or preserving, rehabilitating, or reuniting families;
(4) Preventing or reducing inappropriate institutional care by providing for community-based care, home-based care, or other forms of less intensive care, or

(5) Securing referral or admission for institutional care when other forms of care are not appropriate, or providing services to individuals in institutions . . .[20]

In contrast, Part B is striking.

For the purpose of enforcing the support obligations owed by absent parents to their children, locating absent parents, establishing paternity, and obtaining child support, there is hereby authorized to be appropriated for each fiscal year a sum sufficient to carry out the purposes of this part.[21]

Thus, at a single point in time, Congress passed amendments to the Social Security Act which provided for the broadest social-services programs since the War on Poverty—amendments for which liberals within and outside of two administrations had wrangled—and at the same time set up a second part of the same bureaucratic structure, designed in such a way as to substantially reduce administrative and recipient options vis-à-vis the legal relationship of both to the absent fathers of AFDC-dependent children.

The original legislation, signed with reservations early in 1975 by President Ford, included the following provisions:

1. Established that a Parent Locator Service would be set up within HEW that would have access to such federal data files as those of the Social Security Administration, Civil Service Commission, Defense Department, and the Treasury, in order to facilitate the location of absent parents;
2. Authorized the Internal Revenue Service to use the tax-collection mechanism to enforce the payment of child support;
3. Granted the use of the federal court system to litigate child support cases in the event of inaction at the local or state level;
4. Ruled out bankruptcy as a means of avoiding the child support obligation;
5. Authorized the garnishment of wages of federal employees or those receiving federal or military retirement benefits;
6. Made paternity determination, location, and establishment of support services available to non-AFDC recipients on a sliding-fee basis;
7. Made inclusion of the AFDC grant to the custodial parent contingent upon "cooperation: in the determination of paternity and location process";
8. Established "incentives for local and state participation in the Federal programs" (reimbursement of child support moneys would be in the amount of 25 percent for the first year of the program, set to begin July 1st, 1975, and 10 percent thereafter. In addition, a failure to show cost-effectiveness during yearly HEW audits would lose the negligent state 5 percent of the federal funds to which the state was otherwise entitled as matching for AFDC programs, beginning January 1, 1977);

9. Set formulas for the distribution of child support collections in the following manner:

   a. For the first fifteen months of the program only, 40 percent of the first $50 a month collected would go to the dependant family without penalty;

   b. If the amount collected exceeds the AFDC payment, the additional amount, up to the family's support rights as specified in a court order, would go to the family. If there were still an excess above this, it would be retained by the government to offset past welfare payments. In any case in which a large collection is made that more than repaid all past welfare payments, any such excess would go to the family. The amounts retained by the government would be distributed between federal and state governments according to the proportional matching shares which each had under the AFDC formula (twenty-five percent the first year, 10 percent thereafter of amount collected, net of recipient share, goes to the county, 40 percent of remainder to the state, and remaining 60 percent to the federal government);[22] and

10. Required that AFDC recipients (and non-AFDC recipients choosing to use the support services on a sliding-fee basis) assign their rights to support over to the state, and that states so amend their laws to allow this, in order that the government be granted the legal right to pursue reimbursement of costs associated with location and support, as well as the debt owed by the absent parent to the state for the maintenance of the family.[23]

President Ford's statement of hesitation at signing the bill centered around the "provisions for use of federal courts, tax-collection procedures of IRS, excessive audit requirements and HEW's parent locator service."[24] What followed the bill's signing was months of debate, both within and outside of government, around not only the issues enumerated by President Ford but the following issues as well.

Within HEW, Social Services Commissioner James B. Cardwell was opposed to the release of Social Security numbers to locate absent parents, while the Social and Rehabilitation Service, which was designated in March 1975 to administer the Parent Locator Service, insisted that their release was necessary for the effective functioning of the entire program. Under heavy pressure, and after more than a year's debate, Cardwell reversed his position in April 1976,[25] and HEW Secretary David Matthews authorized the release of the numbers on condition that "confidentiality of the information" be guaranteed by the state program personnel.[26]

The major congressional opposition to the bill as originally signed manifested itself in the summer of 1975, with the Corman-Rangle Bill. The opposition resulted in the following modifications:

(1) Access to the federal courts for adjudication would be limited to those cases certified by the Secretary of HEW or his designee;

(2) The mother would *not* be required to cooperate in identifying or locating a father in the event that the child was a product of incest or forcible rape, or when adoption proceedings were in progress;

(3) Hearings were to be made available to those who felt they had been coerced or whose privacy had been invaded;

(4) The collection services of the IRS would be provided as a last resort and upon certification of the Secretary or his designee, and only in the event the Social Security number and other locational information pertaining to the absent parent were provided by the IV D agency.[27]

By this last provision, the autonomy of the IRS was to an important extent preserved, and the Treasury Department was able to refrain from becoming an instrument in the location of absent parents.

Concerns of opponents however, were not fully abated by the amendments to the bill. The major sponsors who had fought for the legislation for years—Senators Nunn, Russell Long, and Walter Mondale—were said to have held up the confirmation of the nomination of William Howard Taft IV as general counsel of HEW, as leverage to secure the release of the all-important Social Security numbers.[28]

During original Senate hearings for the bill in the fall of 1974, the League of Women Voters' Mrs. Kenneth Greenawalt (National Human Resources chair) was the only representative of the organizations giving testimony who actively opposed the bill in general.[29] Others, including representatives from the National Organization of Women and the Child Welfare League of America, Inc., offered agreement with the bill in principle, but requested that it be made stronger (NOW) or weaker (Child Welfare League) in terms of requirements for compliance and cooperation by various sectors.[30] It should be noted that there were at the time of the hearings two major opposing points of view within the NOW national structure. The NOW representative who gave testimony at the hearings was Betty Spaulding, convenor of the Task Force on Marriage and Divorce. The Task Force on Poverty, whose views were not heard at the hearings, was and remains opposed to much of the legislation on grounds that it is designed in such a way as primarily to harass poor women who request public assistance rather than to pursue child support from men.

One aspect of the legislation which bears discussion deals with the issue of non-AFDC recipient participation in the child support programs. Both NOW and the Child Welfare League, among others, lauded the inclusion of such persons in the original legislation. Due to the predominantly nonpoor makeup of the NOW membership, it is not surprising that this constituency should anticipate greater gains from a new system that would ostensibly be committed to returning greater amounts of child support for less cost than the existing private system had been able to deliver (according to testimony at the hearings). NOW representatives Berry and Spaulding presented evidence to the effect that levels of adjudicated child support and compliance rates over time were quite low, especially when compared with the standard of living to which most nonpoor women, the primary users of the judicial civil system, are accustomed.[31]

Quite naturally, a large segment of the NOW constituency—well-educated, nonpoor women—would welcome a law which would promise more responsiveness and greater benefits than the present system, which relies so heavily upon local judicial discretion in determining child support payment levels,[32] and is handicapped by jurisdictional restrictions and overcrowded dockets. Federalization of child support enforcement, like federal equal employment opportunity laws, would appear, at least on the surface, to provide to women and children an advantage that had never existed before. However, after the initial hearings at which NOW representatives testified in favor of the legislation, the bill as passed called for extending non-AFDC recipient help through July 1, 1976, only one year after commencement of the federal program.[33] As of this writing, the issue of non-AFDC participation as a permanent feature of the program is yet unresolved. Federal officials have decided to continue this feature of the program at least through September 30th, 1978, most likely in order to give them time to assess the impact which non-AFDC recipient participation has upon measurable cost-effectiveness.[34]

The majority of the remaining testimony came from local welfare officials and administrators of state child support enforcement units who, for the most part, spoke in favor of the federal legislation, on grounds that additional collections would be higher than any additional costs incurred as a consequence of the expanded public enforcement effort.[35] There was a conspicuous absence of testimony from the American Civil Liberties Union, which has traditionally concerned itself with helping citizens to protect their right to privacy from the encroachment of government. By August 1975, the ACLU had not yet formulated a policy in response to the legislation, though the organization had noted the progress of the legislation.[36]

Issues

The question remains as to the rationale for the passage of a law which not only entails possible violations of privacy rights, but calls for enormous public expenditure. One assertion appears repeatedly from within the political arena: that costs of AFDC can be dramatically reduced by forcing absent parents to take economic responsibility for their dependent children. And in spite of the fact that favorable testimony regarding the AFDC savings to be anticipated as a result of the federal child support program was *not* well documented, Public Law 93-647 was enacted after very limited public debate. It is difficult to believe that Congress was completely convinced that such a program of child support enforcement would be cost-effective, based upon the poor quality of the testimony given. However, little proof to the contrary was provided, also probably a result of the paucity and inferiority of the available data on the state child support enforcement programs.

It is easier to believe that the bill's potential opponents in Congress, and others who favored the social services provisions (Part A) of Title XX, regarded Part B (the Child Support Enforcement Amendment) as a price to be paid for conservative congressional support for Part A. After all, "logrolling" is not unheard of in these matters. It is also possible that many in Congress perceived the child support provisions as nothing more than innocuous gestures, a "symbolic action," as Murray Edelman has suggested in conversation, which would eventually be emasculated by amendments and reduced to a position similar to that of the WIN programs—that is, administratively costly, but of little economic value to the public. What was underestimated, if this was the case, was the level of commitment on the part of Russell Long's Senate Finance Committee. For at least two years prior to September 1973, as well as can be determined, professional staff members were compiling AFDC and child support data for use by those on the committee in designing the proposed Social Security amendments. For some time there had been close communication between the staff and the administrators of the California child support enforcement programs, which turned out to be the model for the federal law.

This is rather puzzling, in that in spite of testimony by William Knutson, counsel for child support for the California State Department of Social Welfare, that several California "counties collect child support for $.15-$.20 on the dollar,"[37] and a later staff report to the effect that the state of California programs cost twenty-five cents for every dollar collected,[38] the author was told in summer 1975 by Jack Flanders, also counsel for child support in the California Department of Benefit Payments, that there was no central mechanism for keeping track of program costs in California. Administrative costs were not available for the state as a whole, but were available only at the county level. Because of the way in which the California program was structured, the counties were to prepare yearly audits for submission to the county grand juries, which then made funding decisions for the following year. The state kept records on collections, but none on costs. The author was told she would need to go to each county grand jury for a breakdown of administrative costs for location and support programs, and that there was nowhere available at the state level the kind of cost information being sought. The California experience was not atypical at that time. Child support accounting in all of the states which had public enforcement programs was generally very poor prior to implementation of Public Law 93-647.

The legislative history of this particular bill can be traced back at least as far as April 2, 1973, when child support legislation (H.R. 3135) was proposed in conjunction with other Social Security amendments under consideration. As feelings in the House-Senate conference toward the bill as written were generally so negative at that earlier time, the entire package of revisions was abandoned and only an amendment increasing Social Security retirement benefits was signed into law.[39] Long was obviously not deterred by the defeat of the child support provisions, however, and it is important to note his skill as a politician, in that he apparently had decided that the surest way to guarantee passage of a child support enforcement bill would be to attach it to a piece of highly visible, popular legislation. Though this strategy failed in 1973, it was to prove quite successful in 1974, as we have already noted. In much of the testimony and documentation prepared by the Senate Finance Committee staff, the assertion—based upon the positive performance of some of the state child support enforcement programs—was that federalization would lead to reduced AFDC benefits in amounts exceeding the costs of collecting the child support. In its strictest sense, this means that even if collections exceeded costs by only one percent, the program would have been justified. For this reason, policymakers may not have been concerned with the precision of the projected savings. It was apparently enough that the bulk of testimony and data projected no loss. If child support collections do exceed the cost of running the programs, the rationale for the legislation would prove sound. On the other hand, if the public enforcement of the child support obligation were to be viewed as a proper function of government, having intrinsic social value in and of itself, the savings through the reduction of AFDC costs would become a moot issue.

The Empirical Questions

Quite obviously, the philosophical, ethical, and professional issues brought to the fore by the child support program legislation are numerous. In the last chapters we shall address some of these, particularly those confronting policymakers who must decide whether to reduce or expand—and if so, *how* to expand—the public investment in enforcing the child support obligation. The chapters that follow immediately, however, address some of the assumptions that underlie any public system that has as its stated goal the enforcement of the parental support obligation. It is necessary that we first identify the articulated reasons, and possibly the unarticulated beliefs, that form the basis of a public commitment to secure child support from absent parents.

The most frequently encountered argument in favor of this public effort is that it will reduce the taxpayer burden of public assistance. This is to be done by lowering AFDC recipient rates and lowering average grant levels. Inherent in this argument are many other assumptions, among them:

That the fathers of AFDC-dependent children are willingly refusing to support their children rather than economically unable to do so;

That any additional costs of this new administrative effort will be more than offset by the collections to be received; and finally,

That the stability of the family will be fostered, thus reducing the likelihood that a family will be without the support of a male head and dependent upon public support. Many believe that if men were forced to take economic responsibility for their families after a split they would be more inclined to marry the mothers of their children or, if already married, would be less inclined to leave them.[40] (This hypothetical disincentive effect in turn assumes that men are usually the initiators of family formation and dissolution, and that encouraging them to remain at home is less costly in terms of both real and social costs than is doing nothing to discourage them from leaving.)

In addition to the above rationale for enforcing the child support obligation, which focuses on the reduction of AFDC expenditures, other arguments favoring public enforcement are often heard. These include the following:

There is a growing belief that the economic responsibility for children in female-headed families is not equitably shared—that mothers carry a disproportionately greater share of the burden, relative to their ability to do so, than do the absent fathers—and that the private sector has failed to promote a more equitable distribution of that responsibility; and,

There are large numbers of women who maintain intact families that are not conducive to personal growth, and may actually be life-threatening, who would not otherwise do so were they assured of child support; and finally,

Very simply, absent parents *ought* to support their children, and public policy should affirm the right of every child to lay claim to the personal and economic resources of *both* parents.

Although there are other reasons why the public sector might wish to promote a large-scale child support enforcement effort, the above are the reasons most frequently encountered. As can readily be seen, all of these reasons contain assumptions about the nature of human behavior, the extent and distribution of resources, and the measurement of ability to pay which lend themselves to empirical testing. All of these should be answered, but it is beyond the scope of this book to address them all. Therefore, we have chosen to ask and begin to answer what appear to be the most fundamental of these questions.

First, it is necessary to establish a demographic profile of the population of interest—the nonwidowed female heads of families containing children less than eighteen years of age, for whom we might expect child support payments by virtue of that status. Specifically:

1. Nationally, what are their numbers?
2. In what parts of the country do they live?
3. How much education do they have?
4. What races are they?
5. What income do they have?

In addition, we need the same kind of profile of the fathers. We also need to know where they go when the family splits, how many actually disappear, how many form subsequent families, and how much money they earn.

Our second pursuit will be an attempt to identify what appear to be the determinants of levels of child support in the general population. Of those variables commonly held to influence receipt and levels of child support—such as the incomes of both adult parties, remarriage of either, the passage of time, etc.—which ones actually have an impact upon child support? Another important reason for determining the best predictors of levels of child support payments is that policymakers have committed public resources to the enforcement of the support obligation. Efficiency of the new program might possibly be improved by targeting efforts on fathers who possess characteristics associated with higher levels of support, and ignoring those for whom the returns would likely never justify the costs. Although immensely rational, this strategy may be highly questionable if we apply the principle of horizontal equity—that is, that all absent fathers should be subject to the same treatment under the law. This point will be discussed in more detail in later chapters.

The third fundamental issue we will address is that of the extent of resources in the absent father population that might be made available in the form of support payments to their former families. Using two different measures of economic well-being, one based upon earned income and the other upon estimates of earnings capacity, we will address the following questions:

What are the comparative amounts of money which might be viewed as available for the purpose of support? In other words, does the way in which we measure ability to pay have any impact upon how much child support is potentially available?

How much further could support money go toward closing the poverty-income gap of those female-headed households than it does presently?

The fourth substantive question we will examine is that of the potential cost-effectiveness of public child support enforcement programs. Using data from several of the state location and support systems which had been operating before the new federal law took effect, we will derive an estimate of the marginal rate of return on these enforcement programs and take a critical look at the way these figures and other measures of cost-effectiveness have been generated. In addition, we will discuss some preliminary figures from the newly operant federal program.

The final chapters will review our findings, offer suggestions for further research, and discuss some of the problems associated with child support enforcement policy.

Notes

1. Until quite recently, one study has stood alone in this body of legal literature as the only empirical inquiry into levels of, and compliance with, adjudicated child support. The Quenstedt and Winkler study, done in 1964, is repeatedly cited as evidence in support of what family-law practitioners and the courts have observed in the exercice of their profession—that noncompliance with court-ordered support is a serious problem. See Una Rita Quenstedt and Carl F. Winkler, "What Are Our Domestic Relations Judges Thinking?," Monograph No. 1, Section of Family Law, American Bar Association: July 1965.

2. The definitive study by a sociologist of the relationship between a selected set of psychosocial variables and compliance with court-ordered support was first published in 1954. See William Goode, *Women in Divorce,* The Free Press: New York, 1956.

3. Karl de Schweinitz, *England's Road to Social Security,* A.S. Barnes and Company, Inc.: New York, 1943, pp. 27-28.

4. Alvin L. Schorr, *Filial Responsibility in the Modern American Family*, U.S. Department of Health, Education and Welfare: Washington, D.C., 1960, pp. 1-4.

5. Ibid., p. 23.

6. Robert Plotnick and Felicity Skidmore, *Progress Against Poverty: A Review of 1964-1974 Decade,* Academic Press: New York, 1976, p. 91.

7. Maurine McKeany, *The Absent Father and Public Policy in the Program of Aid to Dependent Children,* University of California Press: Berkeley, 1960, p. 4.

8. Ibid., pp. 4-5.

9. Ibid., pp. 60-61.

10. Ibid., pp. 2-3.

11. Heather L. Ross and Isabel V. Sawhill, *Time of Transition: The Growth of Families Headed by Women,* The Urban Institute: Washington, D.C., 1976, p. 102.

12. Frances Fox Piven and Richard A. Cloward, *Regulating the Poor: The Functions of Public Welfare,* Random House: New York, 1971, pp. 150-161.

13. Ross and Sawhill, op. cit., p. 102, and McKeany, op. cit., pp. 2-3.

14. McKeany, p. 66.

15. Ibid., pp. 8-9.

16. Gerald Stouck, "Additional Background on 'Runaway Pappy' Legislation," Office of the President of Wesleyan University: Middletown, Connecticut, January 1975, p. 1.

17. Larry Mead, *Option Paper on Child Support,* Office of Planning and Evaluation, Department of Health, Education and Welfare: Washington, D.C., Spring 1974, pp. 1-2.

18. Honorable Sam Nunn, "Statement Made at the Hearing Before the Committee on Finance," United States Senate, Ninety-third Congress, First Session: September 1973, Washington, D.C.: U.S. Government Printing Office, Stock No. 5270-02021, p. 57.

19. "Dad Net," *The Washington Post,* editorial: June 16, 1975.

20. *An Act, Public Law 93-647,* H.R. 17045, Ninety-third Congress: January 4, 1975, p. 1.

21. Ibid., p. 14.

22. *Summary of the Provisions of H.R. 17045, Social Security and Child Support,* prepared by the staffs of the Committee on Finance, United States Senate, and the Committee on Ways and Means, United States House of Representatives: December 24, 1974, pp. 5-8.

23. "Guidelines for Counties to Request Federal Reimbursement for Child Support and Establishment of Paternity Programs," Wisconsin Department of Health and Social Services: October-December 1975, p. 1.

24. "Federal Role in Finding Absent Fathers, Enforcing Aid Orders Is Signed Into Law," *The Wall Street Journal:* January 6, 1975.

25. "SS Numbers Ordered to Nab Runaway Dads," *Wisconsin State Journal:* April 7, 1976.

26. "SS Numbers Need to Be Confidential for Tracking Fathers," *Wisconsin State Journal:* April 22, 1976.

27. *An Act, Public Law 93-647,* op. cit., pp. 14-24. Also see "Child Support Enforcement Program," *Federal Register,* Vol. 40, No. 124, Part II: Washington, D.C., June 26, 1975, pp. 27154-27169.

28. *Wisconsin State Journal,* op. cit., April 7, 1976.

29. *Child Support and the Work Bonus, Hearing Before the Committee on Finance, United States Senate,* Ninety-third Congress, First Session: September 25, 1973, pp. 212-218.

30. Ibid., pp. 118-134 and 176-212.

31. Ibid., pp. 176-212.

32. John J. Sampson, "Using a Formula to Set Child Support," *Section Report, Family Law,* Vol. 77-1, State Bar of Texas: March 1977, pp. 27-28.

33. *The Social Security Act (As Amended Through January 4, 1975) And Related Laws,* Committee on Finance, United States Senate, U.S. Government Printing Office: February 1975, pp. 250-251.

34. *An Act, H.R. 1404,* Report No. 95-298, Calendar No. 276, Ninety-fifth Congress, First Session: p. 2.

35. There was one exception: Jules Sugarman, administrator of the New York City Human Resources Administration, doubted that a national program such as that being proposed could demonstrate collections in excess of costs. See *Child Support and the Work Bonus,* op. cit.

36. Elizabeth Spaulding, *Comments on the Federal Child Support Enforcement Bills,* NOW Task Force on Marriage and Divorce: August 1975.

37. *Child Support and the Work Bonus,* op. cit., p. 51.

38. *Child Support: Data and Materials,* background information prepared by the staff for the use of the Committee on Finance, United States Senate: November 10, 1975, p. 151.

39. Stouck, op. cit., p. 1.

40. Although we have yet to see it in print or hear it well articulated, we suspect that a similar rationale is applicable to fathers who never live with the mothers of the children they helped produce—that their sexual promiscuity will be curbed, or at least their contraceptive facility will improve, if the associated costs of reproduction are increased. Again, underlying this belief are many other assumptions about the rationality of reproductive behavior and the nature of sexuality itself.

2

Identifying and Describing the Population of Interest: Female Heads of Families Containing Dependent Children

Introduction

The purposes of this chapter are fourfold. We will begin by briefly reviewing recent findings based upon nationwide data from such sources as the Census which describe changes in family headship during the past decade—changes that have resulted in a disproportionate number of female-headed families containing children in the population who are poor. Such changes have also resulted in an increased probability that this type of family will be poor, compared to the case ten years ago.

Second, we will describe the Michigan Panel Study of Income Dynamics, its design, usefulness, and some problems in using data from it, and go on to describe our method of selecting the subsample upon which we focused our subsequent analyses.

Third, we will make some basic comparisons between the Census data and our Michigan subsample data for the purpose of establishing the extent to which the latter are representative.

Finally, we will present a more detailed demographic profile of our Michigan subsample.

The Increasing Incidence of Female-Headed Families in the Population

Among the various changes which have taken place in the demographic character of the American family during the past decade, various researchers have noted a rather dramatic rise in the incidence of families, with children, that are headed by women. Heather Ross and Isabel Sawhill, using data from the 1960 and 1971 Censuses, have identified several factors which have contributed to an increase in the stock of female-headed families during that decade. Among these are:

Changes in Living Arrangements. An increasing proportion of never-married or formerly married mothers are heading their own households rather than living as a subfamily in someone else's household. By 1970, 10 percent more white female heads had chosen to live as separate families, and 8 percent more minority female heads had so chosen, than had been living thus in 1960.

Increased Rates of Marital Disruption. An increasing proportion of ever-married women are separated, divorced, or widowed—a 23 percent increase for whites, 15 percent for minorities over the ten-year period.

Increased Presence of Children. The increased presence of children at the time of marital disruption is attributable to "more divorced or separated women and fewer widows among the maritally disrupted population as a whole";[1] the overall population trend away from childlessness accounted for a 20 percent increase in white female-headed families and a 24 percent increase for minorities.

Higher Illegitimacy. The probability that an unmarried woman will have a child under eighteen living with her accounted for about 15 percent of the growth in the population of female-headed families between 1960 and 1970—9 percent for whites, 21 percent for minorities.

Population Growth. The growth in population alone has resulted in increasing numbers of women currently of childbearing age, adding significantly to the number of those at risk for female headedness. For whites this factor contributed 25 percent of the growth in families headed by women, and for minorities, 16 percent.[2]

As a consequence of the above factors, the Ross-Sawhill study has shown that during the 1960-1970 decade, increasing proportions of all families have female heads.[3] James Sweet's analysis of 1960 and 1970 U.S. Census data complements the findings of Ross and Sawhill. He found that increasing numbers and proportions of children are living in families headed by only one parent. The proportion of children between the ages of zero and five who were living with their mothers only rose from 7 to 11 percent, and for those six to thirteen years of age, from 8 to 12 percent between 1960 and 1970. There were also rises in the percentages of children living only with their fathers during those years, from 0.8 to 1.5 percent in the younger age group, and 1.2 to 2 percent in the older group.[4] It must be stressed, however, that although there is a trend in the direction of more children remaining in the care of their fathers after family dissolution, these numbers remain relatively small. In a study of 458 divorce petitions granted in central Florida from 1971 to 1974, it was found that in only 1.53 percent (seventy) of the cases, custody was awarded to the father.[5] Even more to the point is the fact that the incomes of these single men who head families tend to be higher than those of female heads. Specifically, the U.S. Department of Commerce reported that in 1974, the median annual income of families headed by a female was $6,400, only slightly more than one half (55 percent) of the median annual income of families headed by a male with no wife present, which was $11,740.[6]

Not only do female-headed families with children have lower median incomes than do families headed by males with no wives present, but the former type is exhibiting greater representation over time among the poor. According to Plotnick and Skidmore, in 1965, 32 percent of all poor families were characterized by female headedness, but by 1972, that figure had risen to 47.7 percent![7] Our own analysis of Census data from 1968, 1972, and 1975 confirms both the trend away from the intact, two-parent family and toward the single-parent family (see Table 2-1), and an alarmingly high incidence of poverty among single-parent families containing children less than eighteen years of age (see Table 2-2).

As proportions of families headed by women have grown, so has the probability that such families will be poor. In 1968, as Table 2-2 demonstrates, 43 percent of white female-headed families and 74 percent of all minority female-headed families were poor. In 1972, only four years later, those figures had increased to 48 percent and 75 percent, respectively. As these percentages refer to pretransfer poverty figures, it is likely that part of this increase is attributable to the fact that more women were receiving AFDC and, as a consequence, were working less. By 1975, there had been virtually no change in the frequency with which single-parent families found themselves in poverty,

Table 2-1

Numbers and Percentages of Families Containing Children Less Than 18 Years of Age, by Headship Type and Race

Current Population Surveys, 1968, 1972, and 1975[a]

	1968		1972		1975	
Headship Type	Number	Percent	Number	Percent	Number	Percent
Intact Families:						
White	23,282,479	84	23,648,775	81	23,370,000	78
Minority	2,323,484	8	2,357,965	8	2,497,336	8
Male Heads: (no wife present)						
White	179,648	.64	211,891	.72	347,964	1.17
Minority	55,047	.20	66,831	.23	78,370	.26
Female Heads:						
White	1,211,549	4	1,868,410	6	2,320,000	7.78
Minority	742,059	3	1,141,382	4	1,204,860	4
Total	27,794,266		29,283,705		29,818,530	

[a]The above figures were taken from CPS tapes at the Institute for Research on Poverty, University of Wisconsin. For the purposes of this analysis, the widowed and husband-in-armed-forces categories were eliminated, as we wanted to focus attention exclusively upon a population for whom child support payments were an issue. In addition, families which did not contain children of the head were excluded.

Table 2-2
Percentage of Families[a] with Pretransfer Income-Poverty Ratios Below 1.0 by Race and Type of Headship–1968, 1972, and 1975–Among Those Containing Children Less Than 18 Years of Age

Family Headship Type and Race	*Families with Income-Poverty Ratios 1.0 or Less*		
	Percent in 1968	*Percent in 1972*	*Percent in 1975*
Intact Families:			
White	6.87	6.95	6.84
Minority	23.27	19.62	18.51
Male Heads: (no wife present)			
White	18.26	13.63	13.71
Minority	39.79	35.98	34.51
Female Heads:			
White	43.24	47.52	47.14
Minority	74.23	74.88	70.03

[a]Numbers in each category identical to those in Table 2-1. Similarly, widowed and husband-in-armed-forces categories have been eliminated, as have those families containing children who are not the head's.

with the possible exception of families headed by minority females, which demonstrated a 7 percent reduction (from 74.88 percent to 70.03 percent of that group).

In summary then, in recent years:

1. Increasing proportions of all families containing children less than eighteen years of age are headed by women;
2. Increasing proportions of poor families are headed by women; and
3. Increasing proportions of female-headed families are finding themselves in poverty.

The death of a male head as a reason for female headedness of families containing children under eighteen has become relatively less important in recent years. The probability that a woman in this age range will become a widow has changed little over the last decade, while her chances of becoming divorced, separated, or having an illegitimate child have increased substantially. According to Ross and Sawhill, in 1960, more children (36 percent) lived in families headed by widows than in any other type of female-headed family. By 1970, however, children of both divorced (29 percent) and separated (28 percent) heads outnumbered those of widowed (26 percent) heads, and marital instability had replaced widowhood as the greatest source of the female-headed family.[8]

So not only are we faced with ever-increasing numbers of families headed by women (and women who are increasingly likely to be poor), but these are nonwidows. The importance of this latter fact is that presumably the children in these families have another parent, a father absent from the home, whose earnings might be expected to help prevent or alleviate economic dependence. The extent to which this obligation—that of the absent father to his dependent child—is being and should be discharged is the general topic of the analyses which follow in the remaining chapters. Among the questions to be addressed is not only the extent to which child support payments made by the absent father for the benefit of his dependent children alleviates or prevents poverty status, but also the extent to which child support payments by the absent father help maintain his nonpoor dependent children.

The Michigan Data

As stated in Chapter 1, the purpose of this chapter is to describe our population of interest, female heads of households containing children less than eighteen years of age who would be "eligible" for child support payments. That is, they would be nonwidows whose former spouses are not living with them due to marital disruption or failure of marriage to eventuate with the birth of a child, rather than for reasons such as institutionalization or employment in another geographic area. We use the term "spouse" loosely, as women who were never married to the father of their children are still legally entitled to child support payments from those fathers in most cases.[9] Throughout this book, the terms "husband" and "wife" will be used when such is the reported relationship, though in fact we have no way of knowing the exact legal relationship between adults who cohabit.

In order to be able to extrapolate from our findings based upon analyses of the Michigan data in the following chapters, we will need to know how this population of female heads of families compared with those described in studies based upon Census data.

A small portion of the Michigan Panel Study of Income Dynamics sample was based upon a cross-sectional subsample of poor families previously interviewed by the Bureau of the Census for the Office of Economic Opportunity, and the greater portion was a self-weighting, nationally representative sample, selected by the Survey Research Center at the University of Michigan. The two were combined to produce the original 5,000-family sample. There are several factors which may have contributed to nonrepresentativeness, and subsequent reweighting techniques have been employed to correct for lack of proportional representation in terms of certain demographic characteristics. There has been some concern that the combined weighted sample contains a slightly lower than would be expected proportion of very poor persons (those with incomes less than $1,000 per year). However, the combined weighted Michigan sample compares favorably with the Census data in all other income classes, place of residence, age and sex of family head, race, and number of children under eighteen in the family.[10]

Interviewing for the Michigan Study is done in the early months of each year (usually in person, though lately reliance upon telephone interviews has become the more prevalent practice), and data refer to the calendar year just ended. Thus, 1975 data, the last year available for our analysis, represent information pertinent to 1974. Interviewing is conducted by professional interviewers, and the respondents are compensated with a nominal sum for their cooperation. Although the original Michigan Study sample consisted of 5,000 families, nonresponse and new family formation resulted in a 1975 sample size of approximately 5,600 families.[11] Our subsample of female heads and family splits was drawn from the combined seven-year tape.

Because of the infrequency of the occurrence of men with no wives present who have custody of their dependent children, as well as the relatively high incomes of such families compared with those headed by females, we excluded them from our subsample. Likewise, as our present concern is with child support payments made by an absent father for the maintenance of his dependent child who remained in the custody of the mother following family dissolution, we excluded widows, relatives other than mothers, and other nonrelatives who might have had custody of minor children. It is important to note, however, that future research should focus upon support issues related to children who live with their fathers only, grandparents, or other relatives or nonrelatives, and yet have at least one parent who lives elsewhere. Our decision to focus upon support issues related to the female-headed household and absent father was a practical one, and in no way reflects a value position. To make certain that all children in the household were eligible for child support payments, and no nieces, nephews, grandchildren, or other more distant kin were inadvertently included in the analysis, we required that the family be "nuclear" at the time a woman was identified as eligible for our subsample. As a consequence, we were forced to sacrifice a number of mothers of minor children who were also eligible for child support, but who made their homes with their parents or other relatives or friends.

Three kinds of female-headed families were included in the subsample. First, those families which were already headed by females—single, separated, or divorced—in 1968, the first year of the survey, were selected into the subsample. Second, those female-headed families which emerged as such, because they had originally been subfamily members in the sample or had moved in with sample families and subsequently moved out, or whatever, entered the subsample in the year in which they set up their own female-headed households (1969-1975). Third, "family splits" accounted for additional subsample members. That is, when a husband-wife family, intact during at least one survey year, subsequently separated or divorced, resulting in the wife becoming a female head, she was then included in our subsample. Of this third eligible group, there were two subgroups: Type A, in which the absent spouses were retained in the sample over all subsequent years of the study, and Type B, in which the absent spouses became nonrespondents during subsequent years. Table 2-3 shows how many female heads were identified as subsample members by year and method of identification.

Another primary requirement for enumeration in the subsample was that at least one child be less than eighteen years of age at the time of identification, the assumption being that the legal obligation to support a child ends with his or her attaining the age of legal majority. In the event a child "aged out," rendering the mother ineligible for child support, all data but income, which was inflated, were fixed at that year to permit us to retain that person in the subsample. This was done in only fifty-eight of 578 cases. A set of dummy variables employed for the

Table 2-3
Subsample Membership by Year of Entry Into Subsample

Type of Subsample Member	Number	Percent
Female heads in 1968 when survey was begun (Splits took place in years 1962-1967)	221	38.2
New female heads		
Identified in 1969	16	
1970	22	
1971	25	
1972	29	
1973	25	
1974	21	
1975	26	
Subtotal	164	28.4
New female heads splitting from spouses[a]		
Identified in 1969	12	
1970	20	
1971	40	
1972	27	
1973	25	
1974	26	
1975	43	
Subtotal	193	33.4
Total	578	100

[a]Seventy-five of the former spouses were retained in the Michigan Survey sample after the split, whereas 118 became nonrespondents.

purpose of uncovering any distortions in our empirical analyses as a consequence of this manipulation revealed none. We thus feel certain that the results reported in this and following chapters were not biased by the inclusion of this group. Remarriage of either the female head or the absent father in no way ends the legal right to receive child support or the obligation to pay child support. Thus this change in marital status did not cause these persons to be dropped from our subsample.

We turn now to a comparison of our Michigan subsample of female heads of families and Census data for this type of family, vis-à-vis some important demographic characteristics, bearing in mind the following:

1. Census data were gathered at one point in time, 1974, unless otherwise indicated, whereas our Michigan subsample of female heads were identified as such yearly, from 1968 through 1975. It is thus likely that in spite of weighting procedures employed in the analyses of both the Census data and the Michigan data to make both samples demographically representative of the population at large, there are characteristics of each subpopulation that make them noncomparable. That is, the Census sample of female heads of families in 1974 consists only of that group of people at that one point in time. However, we selected data from a panel study precisely in order that we might measure the effects of certain changes, such as change in marital status, on levels of child support. Therefore, unlike the Census data, our Michigan sample in 1974 includes some remarried women who are no longer heads of families as they were when identified for the subsample in years 1968 through 1974. Thus there is no reason to believe that these populations will be exactly comparable, for a population which contains a portion of remarried women might differ in some indiscernible fashion from one which contains no remarried women; and

2. The criteria used for selecting our subsample from the Michigan data were such that randomness can in no way be assumed. For instance, many families otherwise eligible for child support were excluded from our subsample because of nonnuclear living arrangements which would have caused contamination problems for several of our other measures. We suspect that this fact alone imparted bias to our subsample which we might not have found had we been able to include female heads of subfamilies, for instance, and others not living in nuclear families.

A comparison of our Michigan subsample and a subsample of female heads of families from the Census indicates that, with few exceptions, the two are surprisingly comparable (see Table 2-4). The exceptions include the fact that 44 percent of all minorities in the Census sample live in the South, whereas only 29 percent of all minorities in our Michigan subsample live in that region. Sixty-four percent of all Census minorities are employed, while only 49 percent of all Michigan minorities are employed. In regard to poverty and income measures, one apparent anomaly bears some explanation. A larger proportion of Census respondents received welfare dollars than did the Michigan respondents, but the

Table 2-4

A Comparison of Characteristics of Female Heads of Families that Contain Children Less than 18 Years of Age

U.S. Census and Michigan Survey Data[a]

Demographic Characteristic	Race	1975 Michigan	1975 Census
Place of Residence	All	27	32
(percent living	White	26	26
in the South)	Minority	29	44
Mean Number of	All	2.3	2.3
Children	White	2.2	2.1
	Minority	2.5	2.5
Illegitimacy[b]	All	20	13.0
(Percent)	White	13	6.4
	Minority	39	41.6
Mean Years of	All	11.6	11.1
Education	White	11.8	11.3
	Minority	10.9	11.1
Percent Employed	All	62	66
	White	68	71
	Minority	49	64
Percent Receiving	All	23	45
Public Transfers	White	15	37
(AFDC, food	Minority	41	61
stamps, and/or			
other welfare)			
Mean Cash Value of	All	$3,352	$2,413
Transfers	White	$3,050	$2,395
(For those receiving	Minority	$3,635	$2,416
them only)			

Of Those Not Remarried in 1975:

Mean Annual Earnings[c]	All	$4,724(N=376)	$4,891
Those Employed Only	White	$5,829(N=145)	$5,179
	Minority	$4,030(N=231)	$4,269
Mean Annual Earnings	All	$3,073(N=578)	$3,205
Including the Unemployed	White	$4,380(N=193)	$3,596
	Minority	$2,418(N=385)	$2,492
Percent of Families	All	64.8(N=455)	55
with Pretransfer	White	41.3(N=126)	31
Income-Poverty	Minority	73.9(N=329)	70
Ratios Less than 1			

[a]All Census figures used here, except for those regarding illegitimacy rates, were taken from 1975 Census and Michigan Survey tapes, which are on file at the Institute for Research on

Table 2-4 (cont.)

Poverty, University of Wisconsin-Madison. Unless otherwise indicated, the number of the observations in the weighted subsample of female heads are as follows:

Michigan Data = 4,896,000
 (White = 3,519,000; Minority = 1,376,500)

Census Data from 1975 survey year = 3,524,860
 (White = 2,320,000; Minority = 1,204,860).

[b]These Census figures are percentages of 1973 births which were illegitimate (see footnote 14 to Chapter 2). The Michigan figures include women who had at least one discernible illegitimate child before or during any of the survey years. Thus compatibility is rough, at best. (See following chapter for a description of how legitimacy status was determined.)

[c]Census income is measured for the entire family unit, while the Michigan Survey data allow us to distinguish income by source. Therefore, even though the Census families are headed by females with divorced, never-married, or separated marital status, there may be cases in which income of adult children who are living in the home is included. This could account for some of the discrepancy between the incomes of the two sample groups.

mean payment for those who received payments is higher in our Michigan subsample. This is probably because the percent receiving public transfers includes female heads who remarried in the Michigan subsample, while this is not the case for the Census figures. Thus, a male-headed family would be less likely to receive larger amounts because of its larger size (poor families with male heads are likely to be larger than poor families with female heads).[12] It appears that our subsample of female heads is, generally speaking, a slightly better educated population, with slightly more children and higher illegitimacy rates, especially for whites, and one which is less likely to be living in the South than is the Census subsample, though the two are generally comparable.

In summary then, it is important to bear in mind as our examination of child support phenomena proceeds that this particular population of female heads from the Michigan Survey might be slightly nonrepresentative, if Census data are assumed to be accurately so. However, the two subsample populations are enough alike along the more important demographic dimensions to make us confident that extrapolation from our findings to the general population of female heads of families across the country will be justified.

Notes

1. Heather L. Ross and Isabel V. Sawhill, *Time of Transition: The Growth of Families Headed by Women,* The Urban Institute: Washington, D.C., 1975, p. 23.

2. Ibid., pp. 21-24.

3. Ibid., p. 68.

4. James A. Sweet, *The Family Living Arrangements of Children,* Working Paper 74-28, Center for Demography and Ecology, University of Wisconsin: December 1974, p. 3.

5. Kenneth R. White and Thomas Stone, Jr., "A Study of Alimony and Child Support Rulings with Some Recommendations," *Family Law Quarterly,* Vol. X, No. 1: Spring 1976, pp. 75-91.

6. "Money Income in 1974 of Families and Persons in the United States," *Current Population Reports: Consumer Income,* Series P-60, No. 101: January 1976, p. 2.

7. Robert D. Plotnick and Felicity Skidmore, *Progress Against Poverty: A Review of the 1964-1974 Decade,* Academic Press: New York, 1976, pp. 81-97.

8. Ross and Sawhill, op. cit., p. 132.

9. Martin R. Levy and Elaine C. Duncan, "The Impact of Roe Versus Wade on Paternal Support Statutes: A Constitutional Analysis," *Family Law Quarterly,* Vol. X, No. 3: Fall 1976, p. 181.

10. *A Panel Study of Income Dynamics: Study Design, Procedures, Available Data,* 1968-1972 Interviewing Years (Wave I-V), Vol. 1, Institute for Social Research, University of Michigan: Ann Arbor, 1972, p. 30.

11. Ibid., pp. 27-30.

12. Ross and Sawhill, op. cit., p. 198.

3 Some Determinants of Child Support Payment Levels

Introduction

The recent dramatic rise in the incidence of female-headed families, most of which need income support or supplementation from other sources, quite naturally prompts discussion of alternative strategies for helping to ameliorate the economic problems faced by these families. As stated in chapter 1, however, there are reasons in addition to the possible reduction in income-maintenance program costs that justify taking a closer look at the child support enforcement system. Promoting parental equity and responsibility might be viewed by some as being even more important than reducing the public cost of economic dependence. Whatever the social objectives or their ranking, it is necessary first to determine some facts pertaining to the parameters of the child support phenomenon, to wit:

1. What factors appear to determine how much child support is currently being paid to both the poor and the nonpoor under the present system?
2. How much child support is necessary in order for poor families who are potential recipients to be economically independent of public transfers?
3. How much is the father able to pay toward the support of his children?, and
4. How much will it cost society in real and social terms, to secure what amount of child support from absent fathers?

This chapter will address the first of the above questions, for we presently do not know what factors appear to dominate our public-private system of child support enforcement and what the overall impact of this system is, in terms of support payments, upon female-headed families. It is to be hoped that through this effort we will gain some insight into this phenomenon.

The Theory

Unfortunately, we do not have much in the way of theory or evidence as to the determinants of levels of child support. There are a number of possible types of contributing factors or variables, for instance, legal-system variables as they affect support orders. These might include personal judgments as to the relative guilt or innocence of the parties to a divorce and the punitive use of child

35

support as a consequence of these judgments.[1] Judicial attitudes toward the economic needs and rights of certain classes of citizens, such as whites and minorities, men and women, upper- and lower-income persons, and couples with "conventional" and "nonconventional" life-styles, might also affect levels of child support orders. Additionally, the provisions of the domestic relations laws themselves as they vary from state to state might have an impact on levels of support. For instance, the narrowness of grounds for divorce might, by forcing pretrial collusion between husband and wife, also have the result of forcing up (or down) levels of child support.

Presently, there are few empirical studies of the relationship between characteristics of the courts and levels of child support awards. One study of nine circuit judges in Orange County, Florida, found that each of the nine judges appeared to use his own set of standards for setting support levels, and though each judge was consistent in the application of his own standards, there appeared to be no consistency *between* the judges—consistency which the author believes to be the objective of the Florida statutes. In other words, each judge was apparently ranking the nine case characteristics—estimated financial needs of the wife and of the husband, total assets and liabilities, the number and ages of the dependent children, the net incomes of each party, and the duration of the marriage—in very different ways, though each judge was internally consistent.[2] Such direct evidence of the extensive discretionary power of the courts in determining the level of child support awards is difficult to find in the legal literature, and further research in this area would be quite helpful in the development of a more complete theory as to the determinants of child support. Although we will not be directly measuring these legal-system variables, our predictive models of child support payments will be such that some inferences vis-à-vis the legal system will be possible.

A second group of variables which one would like to examine for its impact upon levels of child support is that having to do with the psychosocial "set" or predisposition of the principal adults. It would be helpful, for instance, to be able to measure a man's commitment or responsibility level at various stages of the marriage cycle and in different classes of persons for the purpose of relating child support to changes in such levels. Among the clues with which we will construct our exploratory model are those provided by William Goode in his pioneer study, *Women in Divorce,* which noted three characteristics of the absent father that contributed to the regularity of child support payments: the ability to pay support (this was measured by the regularity of previous employment, not by the income of the absent father); the relationship with the former wife; and his attitude toward the support payments themselves. (It is important to note that the female head, not the absent spouse, was the respondent in the Goode study. Therefore, the absent father's attributes were really her perceptions of what those attributes were.)[3] However, attitudes such as those measured by Goode are often highly subjective, and consequently of questionable reliability. Thus, we are faced with the choice of listening to what people report their preferences to be, or inferring their preferences from behavior. Although we prefer and will rely primarily upon the latter, some of the independent variables we will be using in our models may allow us to infer that some attitudes or preferences have an impact on the payment of child support.

The third group of variables which should be examined as it might impact levels of child support is, in fact, more readily accessible than either group above. The variables within this group include the economic and demographic measures traditionally used by social scientists to provide clues as to the nature of a social process. Arthur Young and Company, when studying the relative success of the state location and support programs which pre-dated the new federal programs, was able to discern several absent-father characteristics that were associated with the successful enforcement of the child support obligation.[4] Among these were:

1. Income—public child support collections were more likely if absent fathers had average incomes rather than low or high incomes;
2. Age—although the company found a positive relationship between age and the ease with which absent fathers were located, there was no such relationship between age and the successful collection of support;
3. Employment status—an absent father who was unemployed was a poor risk for support collection;
4. Criminal history—absent fathers with prior criminal records did not pay as great a proportion of their support obligations as those without such records;
5. Occupation—those occupations not unionized or not involving substantial penalties for job mobility showed the lowest probability for successful location but, once located, had higher collection potential;
6. Quality of the marital relationship—there was no demonstrable association between the type or duration of the prior relationship and the percent of the support obligation paid by the absent father;
7. Number of children—the number of children for whom support was expected did not affect the probability that the absent father would fulfill his obligations;
8. Legal status—the amount of support due and the percent paid during the three-year case history were higher when a civil court decree had been issued than if voluntary agreements had been reached or criminal court orders had been handed down;
9. Race—although an association was found between race and the relative difficulty of the location process (only 35 percent of minorities were located, 51 percent of whites), no relationship between race and support compliance was reported;
10. Remarriage—where the absent father had responsibility for providing sup-

port outside the enforcement case in question, either by previous marriage or by marriage or remarriage following estrangement from the mother of the dependent children, the probability of successful location was increased. However, no information was available on support compliance and current family status.[5]

Another study of the determinants of child support payments, by David Chambers, focused upon a random sample of 411 divorce cases involving child support awards in Genesee County, Michigan. Using multiple classification analysis, the variables which Chambers found to explain the greatest amount of variance in the father's payment performance were:

1. Length of the marriage up to the point of separation, with those having been married ten years or more demonstrating significantly better payment performance;
2. Occupation. Managers, professionals, and auto industry workers demonstrated significantly better payment performance than others, while blue-collar workers in nonauto industries showed significantly lower payment performance;
3. The number of children for whom the support was awarded; and
4. The age of the father at the time of the divorce. Those men who were less than forty-one demonstrated significantly better payment performance than did those who were forty-one or older.[6]

Though based upon limited geographic populations, both the Young and Chambers studies have added valuable clues toward the development of an overall model for ascertaining the determinants of child support payments for the population as a whole. When viewed in conjunction with the research findings of William Goode and White and Stone, some important patterns appear to be emerging, to wit: If variables used in all four of these studies were to be placed in a "supply-side," "mediating" (as used here, refers to the legal/judicial/ enforcement system), or "demand-side" category, the two former categories would seem to dominate a predictive model, while the demand for child support appears to have little impact. Due to the limited number and size of the geographic areas from which the sample populations were selected, however, we are unable to extrapolate to the general population of the United States from these four studies, as we have no evidence of the extent to which these sample child support cases were representative.

In addition to the problem of nonrepresentativeness of these four studies, none of them includes a true cross section of individuals who are eligible for child support. That is, we might think of the child support-eligible population as being composed of two parts: those who enter the enforcement system, by either the private-sector route or the public-sector route; and those who do not enter it at all, though they are technically eligible by virtue of having in their homes children whose natural or adoptive fathers do not live with them. It would be useful to know the determinants of child support for a population which includes both of these types of eligibles.

Finally, many aspects of the child support system, which is a dynamic, rather than a static, phenomenon, cannot be captured in research which measures variables at only one point in time. Panel, or longitudinal, studies of the same sample population provide the only means by which many variable relationships can be fully explored.

Because we still have incomplete information as to what in fact determines levels of child support in the population as a whole, our predictive models will of necessity include a great many variables which we have reason to believe *might* have an impact upon child support levels—some of which have been suggested by previous research, but most of which we will be exploring for the first time.

The Predictive Models

It appears useful to look at predictors of levels of child support from several perspectives. First, we would want to know which of the aforementioned types of variables—legal-judicial, psychosocial, and demographic—have an effect upon whether or not child support is being paid at all, and second, which ones appear to impact the amount of child support being paid (totally and per child). Also, we might wish to ascertain the impact of time itself on levels of child support. It has been suggested that there is a tendency for child support payments to decline over time, often disappearing altogether.[7] Finally, there are many reasons to believe that the child support phenomenon varies a great deal by race. The experience of whites and minorities in this country has been different in so many respects—economically, educationally, legally, psychologically, and so forth—that it is naive to believe that the same predictive model for child support applies to whites and minorities. To include both in one model could lose us a great deal in terms of accuracy and clarity. Therefore, much of our analysis will focus upon our Michigan Panel Study subsample, divided on the basis of minority-majority status.

In summary, we will be testing one basic regression model on populations divided as described above, and then combining those populations and using three variations of the model (in the form of three different dependent variables) for a total of nine regression equations. See Table A-21 in the Appendix for description of the basic regression equation employed in this analysis. In general, our model for both populations states that child support is a function of the income of both parents, their taste for securing a particular life-style for themselves and their offspring, the operation of the legal apparatus for securing child support, and the number of dependents between which resources must be divided.

The Data

Our subsample families for whom child support is to be expected were identified as a consequence of female headedness. As detailed earlier in chapter 2, female-headed families containing children less than eighteen years of age from the Michigan sample were selected into our subsample by three different methods (see Table 2-3). In only one of these instances did we have complete demographic information on the fathers of the children. These were the family splits families which were intact during at least one of the survey years. In the event our subsample members were already female heads of families in the base year of the Michigan Survey, or moved out of sample families in which they had been subfamilies, most of the measures relating to their former spouses were assigned values of -1 in order that we might account for the impact of this data being missing. The variables treated thus included the absent father's current wife's income, his current marital status, his education, occupation, place of residence, and the number of children in his current family unit. The exceptions were income, which was estimated from the mean of the absent fathers for whom we had current income data, and race, which was presumed to be the same as that of the female head.

Description of the Measures[8]

The Dependent Variables

1. Average Amount of Child Support. Average child support was the average amount of child support *per child* received by the mother during the previous year. For example, $300 in child support payments was recorded as $300, $150, and $100 for families with one, two, and three children, respectively. Unfortunately, the Michigan Survey question regarding the amount of support received failed to distinguish between child support and alimony. Technically and legally, there are some important distinctions between the two. In practical terms this distinction may be meaningless, for reasons we shall discuss later.

2. Total Child Support. This was the total amount of child support received by a female-headed family in 1975.

3. Receipt of Child Support. Receipt of child support was a dummy variable, zero if no child support was received, and one if any child support at all was received.

The Independent Variables

4. Absent Spouse/Father's Nontransfer Income. This variable represented the total income from earnings, investments, and assets for the spouse. In the event that we had no current income measures for the study year due to his attrition from the sample following a split, his income was inflated from the last survey year in which he was interviewed. If we never had data on the absent spouse, as in the cases of those who were female heads of families in 1968 and those who were former subfamiliy members, income was estimated from the mean for the "family splits" absent spouses.

5. Absent Father's Current Wife's Nontransfer Income. This was a continuous measure of the income of the absent spouse's subsequent wife, in the event he had remarried. If he had not remarried the year the dependent variables were measured, or if no absent spouse record was available, -1 was the assigned value. Zero was applicable only in the event that an absent spouse had remarried but his current wife had no income. This measure included earnings and income from interest and dividends only.

6. Female Head's Nontransfer Income. This was measured exactly as was that of the absent spouse. No estimation or inflation was necessary, however, for the female heads because they were our subsample members and, as survey respondents, always had reported income of zero or greater.

7. Female Head's Current Husband's Nontransfer Income. In the event out subsample member had remarried, her current husband's income was measured just as the above, in continuous amounts, beginning with zero. However, if she had not remarried, the recorded amount was -1.

8. Number of Years Since Split. This continuous variable was available on the data file for those who were female heads in the initial survey year, 1968, but had to be created, based upon the year the split occurred, for the others. For these, the year of the split was the survey year in which they first emerged as female heads of families.

9. Female Head Remarriage. This is a dummy variable measured in the same year that the dependent variables were measured. Thus, if a female head in 1968 remarried and divorced prior to 1975 (the year in which the dependent variables were measured), we were unable to take account of this. It was only the presence of a current spouse in the same year that child support was being measured of which we took note.

10. Absent Father's Remarriage. Similarly, the fact of subsequent family formation on the part of the absent spouse was only noteworthy at the time the dependent variables were measured.

11. Absent Father's Education. This was a continuous variable ranging from zero to eighteen and including postgraduate-level education for two years beyond the bachelor's degree. This was measured at the year before the split in the case of family splits, and the mean for this group of absent fathers was attributed to those for whom this information was missing.

12. Female Head's Education. This was measured exactly as that of the absent spouse.

13. Female Head's Occupation. We developed a series of five dummy variables which represented the following categories: professionals, managers, and self-employed business women; clerical and sales workers; crafts workers, operatives, farmers, and ranchers; unskilled laborers and service workers; and unemployed.

14. Absent Father's Occupation. Identical to the above (Variable 13).

15. Absent Father's Residence. This was a dummy variable which measured whether the absent father's place of residence was the same state or a different one from that of the female head at the time the dependent variables were measured. This variable applied only to the cases in which the absent spouse was interviewed in years following the split, and did not apply in the cases in which this information was not available, when it was recorded as −1.

16. Absent Father Retention. Similarly, absent father retention was a dummy variable designed to capture the effect of attrition of the absent father from the sample following the split (−1 for absent fathers who were never subsample members), and might be viewed as a proxy for high mobility, transience, or unwillingness to maintain former associations.

17. Non-South. This dummy variable was designed to capture the effect of the female head's region of residence upon the dependent variables.

18. Race (White). This was a dummy variable which was dichotomized into white and minority to capture the effect of majority or minority status. Because there were only thirteen respondents who identified themselves as Hispanics and three as Asian-Americans, it would have been statistically impossible to ascertain the effects of these two categories. Thus, they were subsumed into the minority category along with those who classified themselves as Negro.

19. Welfare Status. Also a dummy variable, the AFDC status of the female head was measured at the same point in time as the dependent variables were measured.

20. Total Amount of Means-Tested Transfers. Amount of transfers, as distinct from AFDC status (Variable 19), referred to the sum of the cash value of food stamps, AFDC, and other welfare, usually emergency assistance.

21. Illegitimate Status of Children. This measure, a dummy variable, applies only to the children for whom child support is an issue in this analysis (see Variable 22). Thus, an illegitimate child born after a split was not measured by this variable. In the event that a woman's marital status was single, separated, or divorced the year of a child's birth and the prior year, the child was assumed to be illegitimate. Thus we might expect an underestimate of illegitimacy.

22. Number of Children in Each Female-Headed Household for Whom Child Support was Expected. This variable measured the number of children under eighteen in the family unit at the time the female head was identified as eligible for our subsample. No children born more than one year later were included in this measure, even if a second marriage and split was observed during the survey years. Thus, only one man was assumed to have fathered the children she had at the time a female head was enumerated in our subsample, and, in the case of family splits, only one father's demographic characteristics appear on her file. Consequently, double counting problems were avoided, but at the price of possibly inflated estimates of per-child levels of support. It was our opinion, after scrutinizing the files of many subsample members, that the phenomenon of remarriage, childbirth, and yet another split during the survey years occurred very infrequently and not enough to impart significant bias to our results.

23. Age of Youngest Child at Time of Split. This was a straightforward, continuous measure except in the case of children who were quite young at the time of the split. As a consequence of the Michigan Survey interview practice of recording the age of any child newly born (zero) through twenty-three months of age as one year old, together with the varying spring interviewing schedule, it was possible that a child could be "one year old" for three interview years. What was more likely was that a child was "one year old" for two years. Nevertheless, this distortion helps account for the fact that a very large proportion (48 percent) of our subsample had a child "one year old" at the time of the split. Consequently, one should think of this category as "a child less than two years of age." Another factor contributing to such a high frequency was the large number (164) of young women who entered our subsample when they moved out of their parents' homes upon the birth of their first, and usually illegitimate, child.

24. Number of Children in the Current Family Unit of the Absent Father. This continuous variable was measured at the same point in time as the dependent variables, but has a zero-to-ten value only in the case of absent fathers who were retained after a split. The mean value for this group was attributed to absent fathers who had disappeared from the sample. Unlike the measure for the number of children born to the female head following the split (Variable 21), there was no method, given the way in which the interview questions were worded, to discern which children in a man's current household were his own natural or adopted children and which were the products of his current wife's former union, for instance. Thus children included in this measure could have been either or both. As we required that the family be "nuclear" at the time this variable was measured, no other, more distant relationships were possible, however.

25. Missing Data Dummy. If an absent father was not a sample member in 1974, there were missing data for all variables but race, which was presumed to be the same as that of the female head, and income, which was estimated from the mean of absent fathers for whom we had income measures. This variable for missing data served to capture the effect of having no other demographic information on the absent spouse (−1).

Expected Results

In terms of our general model, we expected the following:

1. That for both the white and minority populations of female heads, the four income measures—those for the two principals and their current spouses, if any—would be the best predictors both of levels of child support, and of whether any or none was received. However, it was expected that the coefficients would differ in the following way: Unlike the coefficient for the absent father's income, the sign for the coefficient of the female head's income could have been in either direction. On the one hand, the higher her income, the greater her ability to purchase a high quality (and quantity) of legal services. On the other hand, the higher her income, the less she would need to pursue higher child support payments, and the less family court judges might be inclined to award.

2. We expected that the number of children in a family who were eligible for child support would be a positive, significant predictor of the total amount of child support, and that this would reflect the extent to which absent fathers respond to increasing needs of larger families with greater amounts of child support. However, we expected the coefficient to be negative when the dependent variable was average (per child) amounts of support, reflecting increasing economies of scale. When the dependent variable is the dummy for receipt/nonreceipt of child support, however, we predicted that the number of children would have no impact upon whether or not child support was received, controlling for all other factors.

3. We expected that current family status of the absent father would be significantly related to levels of child support in that current family needs (e.g., a new family) would take priority over children from the former family. We expected this to be a consequence of both the absent father's preferences and

judicial discretion. Likewise, in the event that the female head remarried we expected child support to be depressed, as judges and former spouses would assume income from her current spouse to be available to the children of her former union, regardless of prescriptions to the contrary. Also, the portion of the dependent variable which represented alimony would be reflected in a negative coefficient when the dependent variable was either of the continuous measures. When the dependent variable was receipt/nonreceipt of child support, a negative coefficient would reflect the extent to which all payments cease with remarriage, and a positive coefficient would reflect the extent to which remarriage of the female head engenders payments when none were previously forthcoming. This latter could happen if remarriage embarrassed a nonpaying father, or it could mean that the personal characteristics of the female head that are associated with remarriage are the same as those associated with her greater ability to make the child support enforcement system work better on her behalf.

4. Age of the youngest child at the time of the split could produce a coefficient with either a negative or a positive sign. On the one hand, a judge might award a woman with a very young child larger support to reward her for remaining (or to encourage her to remain) at home with her child rather than going to work outside the home. On the other hand, a woman whose youngest child was a teenager at the time of the split had greater food, shelter, and clothing expenses for that child and consequently, all other things being equal, might have been awarded larger support payments. Also, assuming a high positive correlation between the age of her youngest child and the duration of the marriage, high support awards especially as this measure included alimony, could partially represent a reward for "length of matrimonial service."

5. We expected the coefficients for our (continuous) education measures for both fathers and female heads to be significant and positive, even while controlling for income, for reasons related to acculturation and value orientation. That is, the longer a person remains within the educational system, the more likely he or she is to acquire a sense of responsibility for the consequences of individual deeds. This increases the likelihood that the absent father will pay support and that the female head will possess the knowledge, values, and competence to seek enforcement of support through the courts.

6. Likewise, we expected our set of dummy variables representing the highest occupational levels to be both positive and significant for female heads. The higher the position a female head occupied, the more likely she would be to have the understanding or ability to maneuver within the legal system in order to facilitate higher levels of child support. The coefficients for absent fathers' higher occupational rankings could have either sign, however. On the one hand, he could be exposed to greater peer pressure to provide support, the higher his occupational status. On the other hand, very high status could afford him the opportunity to negotiate lower levels of support, all other things being equal.

7. We anticipated that the effect of an absent father's attrition from the

sample following a family split would be negative. This would not be the case in the event the attrition were attributable to the Michigan Study team's poor retrieval efforts, which is unlikely. However, if post-split attrition from the sample is indicative of high mobility, marginal attachment to the labor force and other stabilizing institutions, or even avoidance of child support, our predictions would be confirmed. One finding of the Young researchers, it will be recalled, was that support compliance was higher if a man held a job or belonged to a union which imposed high costs for mobility.[9]

8. We expected child support payments to be lower if the absent father's residence were in a state other than that of the female head. This is due to the legal requirements governing courts of jurisdiction and limitations in the Uniform Reciprocal Enforcement of Support agreements. Proximity might also be either an *indication* of greater interest in a man's children or the *cause* of greater interest in his children. A man may choose both to remain geographically close to his children after a split and to pay higher amounts of child support as a function of his love and concern for them. Similarly, a woman may choose not to move the children to a different locale as a consequence of the affectional and/or economic ties they have with their father. Frequent visits with his children are more convenient, and therefore more likely, if a man lives closer to them. If child support payments are, in part at least, perceived by him as a cost of the privilege and pleasure of being with them, a positive sign for the residence coefficient would also result.

9. In spite of the fact that being a public assistance recipient implies low earnings relative to need, we expected that the coefficient for this dummy variable would be positive, reflecting the legal and administrative resources brought to bear upon the task of securing child support. We expected the coefficient to be larger for our white population, however, reflecting bias within the welfare system in relation to the perceived characteristics of white and minority fathers—the latter being perceived as less responsible and therefore less likely to contribute support once the legal obligation was established.

10. Amount of welfare, on the other hand, we expected to produce a negative coefficient, reflecting the extent to which the income-need deficit of the family is offset by public transfers, which might be viewed as a substitute for child support. This is actually the case in many states where child support, as unearned income, reduces the AFDC grant dollar for dollar. Because the higher support payments were, *ceteris paribus,* the less likely it would be that the female head would receive welfare and the smaller the welfare payments would be, the coefficients of the dummy and the continuous welfare measures must be viewed with some caution.

11. There are a number of reasons why we expected the coefficient for region (non-South) to be positive, especially for minorities. To the extent that commonly held beliefs about the rigid conservatism, racism, and sexism of southerners are true and reflected in the judicial system, the child support

awards would be lower, especially for minorities. If southerners are more racist than others, and the southern legal/judicial/enforcement system reflects a prevailing racist stereotyping of minority families as having lower economic needs than the white majority, then the non-South coefficient will be larger for the minority subsample. For both populations living outside the South we expected higher child support, all other things being equal, because northern and north central states have experienced higher family dissolution rates,[10] and therefore should have developed more equitable and efficient systems for enforcing the child support obligation.

12. We expected the fact of a child's being illegitimate to negatively impact the child support coefficient because of the reduced likelihood that the father could be legally identified as such and/or held financially responsible for the child. As recently as 1973, the Supreme Court declared unconstitutional a Texas statute which denied the right of the illegitimate child to be supported by his or her father.[11]

13. The number of years which had passed since the couple split up, either because of divorce, separation, or the failure of marriage to eventuate with the birth of a child, we expected to produce a negative coefficient for all of the dependent variables for both populations. This we predicted would be the consequence of devaluation of the child over time by the absent father, and increasing costs, relative to benefits, of repeated litigation in pursuit of regular payments on the part of the female head.

14. Race, included as a variable in the model when we combined the white and minority populations, we expected would be positive and significant, for the reasons suggested earlier.

Limitations of the Model

It is apparent, due to limitations inherent in the data set itself, that there were a number of variables which could not be included in our model. Among these were those that relate directly to the legal system and use patterns thereof, and direct personal or psychological measures of the absent father vis-à-vis criteria he might use for deciding how much child support to pay.

The overall value of the model lies in the contribution it makes to our understanding of the ultimate impact of the child support enforcement system, both qualitatively and quantitatively, across the United States today.

Findings

There were many surprises resulting from the tests of our model. As can be seen in Table 3-1, there were fairly large differences for the three sample populations

Table 3-1

Amount of Variance Explained by the Model by Population Type and Dependent Variable, in Percentages

| Sample Population Type | Dependent Variable | | |
	Receipt of Child Support	Total Amount of Child Support	Average Per Child Amount of Child Support
White	24	34	37
Minorities	16	16	10
Combined	23	31	34

in the total amounts of variance in child support which was explained by the model. The model was least helpful in predicting the payment or level of child support for minorities (N_m = 385), and best for whites (N_w = 193), especially when the dependent variable was average child support payment. When the two populations were combined a greater amount of the total variance was explained by the model for all three dependent variables than when the subsample population consisted only of minorities, but slightly less when it was white. This suggests that:

1. Our model is better able to capture the factors which contribute to the payment (and nonpayment) of child support among whites than it is among minorities; and

2. Many differences in the effects of the variables in the model upon the two populations might well have been obscured had we not separated them. Before moving on to a discussion of the results for the two separate populations, however, a brief discussion of the results for the combined populations is in order.

It will be recalled that the model, run with the three different dependent variables, was identical for the combined population except that a dummy variable, race, was included. Table 3-2 lists the statistically significant variables for the white, minority, and combined populations when the dependent variables were receipt/nonreceipt and total amount of child support. See Tables A-4 through A-12 in the Appendix for a complete reporting of the regression results including those for the dependent variable, Average (per child) Support. The t-values for race were the largest of any in the model—4.96 when the dependent variable was the dummy receipt/nonreceipt, 5.47 when it was total amount, and 4.54 when it was average (per child) amount.

The fact of being white, then, all other things being equal, accounted for an increment of nearly $413 in the total yearly amount of support. Considering that our average amount of support for the combined population is only $863, this is a dramatic difference.

The White and Minority Populations

In addition to interpreting our regression results in terms of minority or majority status, it is helpful to pay especially close attention to both the magnitude and the direction of the coefficients. Just as much valuable insight into the dynamics of the child support phenomenon can be lost by combining whites and minorities in the same study population, in a model-testing exercise of this sort it is important to look closely at results in a manner which goes beyond a focus upon statistical significance. This is particularly true in the case of a rather limited sample size and a large number of variables. This point will hopefully be made clearer as we elaborate on our findings.

In terms of high levels of statistical significance, Table 3-2 does suggest in fact, that both the receipt and level of child support payments were determined by different factors for whites and minorities. The income of the minority absent father was a highly significant determinant of whether or not any support was contributed to his former family and, if so, the extent of that contribution. (It is very important to keep in mind that this regression model allows us to account for the impact upon the dependent variable of changes in one independent variable, while holding constant the values of the other variables. Thus, when we say that income has a given effect, this means that the effect is attributable to income alone and not to an interaction between income and some other variable, such as occupation, which is included in the equation.) The income of white absent fathers was a significant determinant only of levels of support, however, and not of whether or not any payment was made. For both sample populations, over four cents in child support was contributed for every additional dollar the absent father earned.

Another independent variable which was of statistical significance for both populations was the dummy variable for missing data. It will be recalled that after a family split, some absent fathers disappeared from the sample. It will also be recalled that some of their characteristics, such as race, could be considered constant or permanent, while others, such as current marital status, were often unknown in the year in which the dependent variables were measured. Our results showed that the fact of having no current information about the absent father was a highly significant determinant for both whites and minorities, of whether or not any support at all was received in 1974, but for neither population did it have a significant impact upon levels of support. If this variable is viewed as a proxy for high mobility (both occupational and geographical), then our results might be seen as consistent with the Young findings pertaining to their sample of enforcement cases.

Table 3-2
Variables that Have a Significant Impact Upon Child Support, by Sample Population Type and Dependent Variables (Receipt/Non-receipt and Total Amount Only)

Population Type	Receipt/Non-receipt			Total Amount		
	Variable Name	Regression Coefficient	Significance Level	Variable Name	Regression Coefficient	Significance Level
Combined	Absent Father's Income	.00002 (Standardized .1476)	.01		.049	.01
	Female Head Remarriage	−.1447	.01		−292.33	.01
	Absent Father's Retention	−.2306	.01		−406.10	.01
	Race (White)	.2021	.01		412.82	.01
	Missing Data (Dummy)	−.2450	.01		−513.18	.01
				Absent Father's Wife's Income	.071	.05
				Absent Father's Remarriage	489.41	.01
				Absent Father's Occupation I	312.99	.05
				Absent Father's Occupation III	354.35	.05
				Absent Father's Residence	385.23	.05
				Number of Children Eligible for Support	47.39	.05

Minority				
Absent Father's Income	.00003 (Standardized .2391)	.01	.042	.01
Absent Father's Occupation I	-.0108	.05		
Absent Father's Residence	.3149	.05	379.95	.05
Missing Data (Dummy)	-.2345	.05		
Female Head Remarriage	-.0977	.01	-684.46	.01
White				
Absent Father Retention	-.2416	.05	-540.04	.05
Missing Data (Dummy)	-.2784	.05		
Absent Father's Income			.054	.05
Absent Father's Remarriage			726.80	.05
Number of Children Eligible for Support			152.44	.05

With the exception of the missing data dummy, and the absent father's income, the independent variables which had a significant effect upon both receipt and levels of support differed between the white and minority sample populations. Minority absent fathers who were professionals or otherwise fell into our highest occupational classification were significantly less likely to be contributing any support, controlling for all other factors, than were those in the other occupations. This is a puzzling result.

The final independent variable in the model which was of statistically significant importance for the minority population was the residence of the absent father. In the event a minority father lived in the same state in which his children and their mother lived, he was not only more likely to have contributed support, but that support was about $380 higher than the support contributed by minority absent fathers who lived in a different state than the mother and children. This may reflect problems in the system for the enforcement of an interstate support obligation, but it may also be viewed as a proxy for a man's diminished interest in his children who live far away.

Turning now to the most statistically significant determinants of receipt and levels of child support for the white sample population, we found that if the female head remarried, not only was the amount of support likely to be reduced by $684 per year, but it was quite likely that it ceased altogether! Although one might expect some decrease in support with her remarriage due to the elimination of the alimony portion, there should not have been a total cessation of support, especially to such a significant extent. To obtain a crude estimate of the proportion of the decrement which is due to the cessation of both types of payment—child support and alimony—we multiplied the mean payment for those who pay something, $1,467, by the coefficient for female head remarriage, −.3025, which equals $443.77. This result suggests that about $204.69, or slightly less than one third of the reduction in support paid by white men in our subsample, might be attributable to the cessation of the alimony portion of the measure.

Whether or not a white father was retained in the sample after the family split was a statistically significant predictor of both the level of support and whether any support at all was received by the dependent family. In the event he was lost from the sample, which could be interpreted as a proxy for his wish to abandon former ties and associations, we found that fully $540 less was received by his children and their mother in the form of support.

Perhaps one of the biggest surprises of our model-testing was to be found in the direction of the coefficient for absent father's remarriage for the white sample population. Although it was not statistically significant when the dependent variable was receipt/nonreceipt, the level of support *increased* by almost $727 in the event an absent father had remarried! Contrary to popular belief then, our evidence suggests that for the white population, having a subsequent family may actually improve a man's child support payment performance, though it is not likely to increase the probability that he will pay anything at all if he is presently paying nothing. The increase in the total amount of the support is so large, in fact, that it more than offsets the loss sustained by the coefficient for remarriage of the female head. The per child amount also increases significantly—$458—for this sample population. See Table A-12 in the Appendix.

This point aside, one can speculate as to the reasons for this totally unanticipated effect. Why should the fact of the absent father's remarriage account for such a large increase in the level of child support, all other factors—including the new wife's income—held constant? Two possible explanations occurred to us. First, it is possible that the sort of person who is inclined to form close attachments to and take responsibility for others, as manifest by marriage, feels more responsibility toward his children and thus pays higher and more regular support than a man who is not inclined to remarry. A second possibility is that the subsequent wife encourages his payment of child support, either directly or indirectly, by alleviating any inclination he might have to punish the former wife by withholding regular child support payments. As the fact of remarriage and the dependent variables were measured simultaneously, we have no way of ascertaining the correct causal link between remarriage and the payment of support.

The number of children who were eligible for child support did not have a statistically significant impact upon whether or not any support at all was received in the study year, but it was highly significant as a predictor of the total amount of support which was received. For every additional eligible child, a white absent father contributed $152 more. When the dependent variable was average (per child) support, however, the coefficient, as predicted, bore a negative sign, indicating that each additional child in the dependent family had the effect of lowering the average amount each would receive. Though not statistically significant at the .05 level, we have confidence that this pattern is a consistent one for both sample populations, for reasons which will be discussed later.

In summary, then, in many respects the model which best explains child support performance for minorities is different from that which best explains support performance for whites. While income, occupation, and geographic proximity to his children were the best predictors for the minority father, remarriage, income, and number of child support-dependent children were the best predictors for the white population.

As mentioned earlier, it is often of great value, especially when engaged in an exploratory effort such as the present one, to look for clues to the nature of a phenomenon that lie beyond strictly delimited levels of statistical significance. This is because confidence in research results is a rather relative issue. That is, though we have enormous confidence in results which are likely to occur 95 percent of the time, we are not totally lacking confidence in results which occur, say, only 60 percent of the time. Because we believe there to be some merit in looking more closely at less statistically significant results, we will proceed with a discussion which focuses upon the direction and relative magnitude of our results.

We find, for instance, that all but one of the coefficients for the income of the absent father's current wife were positive, as predicted. (The exception occurred for the minority population when the dependent variable was average child support payment. For complete documentation of our results see Tables A-4 through A-12 in the Appendix.) Furthermore, when the dependent variable was receipt/nonreceipt the t-values were only .02 and 1.33 for the white and minority populations respectively, which suggests that the impact of the absent father's current wife's income may be stronger for minorities than for whites. The size of the coefficient for minorities suggests that each additional dollar which this wife earns might increase the amount of support which the absent father's former family receives by about seven to nine cents, controlling for all other factors in the model. The direction and magnitude of the coefficients for each population suggest in general that for whites, a subsequent wife's income has no bearing on whether or not her husband contributes support to his former family, but if so, the total will most likely increase by about seven cents for every dollar of her income. On the other hand, for minorities a subsequent wife's income *does* have some impact on whether or not her husband contributes to the support of children from a prior marriage, and also has the effect of increasing total support by about nine cents for each additional dollar she earns.

It will be recalled that earlier in this chapter we predicted that the sign of the female head's income coefficient could be either positive or negative. More income would on the one hand enable her to purchase better legal services and consequently obtain higher payments. We found that the signs for all the coefficients for female head's income were negative, for both whites and minorities. However, the size of the coefficients was so small that we have no confidence that the negative signs mean much in terms of our predictions. As a matter of fact, it is likely that the contrasting effects which were predicted were both operant, and this could explain the low coefficients for this variable.

Similarly, female head's husband's income (in the event she was one of the 123 female heads to remarry) produced coefficients with signs both positive and negative for both sample populations, though the t-values associated with these coefficients were exceedingly small and thus not statistically significant. It is likely that the explanation for these low coefficients is the same as that for the low coefficients for female head's income.

Perhaps the biggest surprise of our model-testing exercise was that the number of years since the couple split had little impact on the dependent variables, and not always in the expected direction. This is surprising because it flies in the face of all common knowledge as well as what tentative evidence there is on the subject. Contingency table analysis was run on a crosstab of number of years since the split and amount of child support. The results were not even marginally significant (X^2=135.75 with 132 df's), and convinced us that our regression findings were in fact reliable. See Tables A-2 and A-3 in the Appendix for these results. What we discovered was that although the sign of the coefficients was in the predicted direction (negative) for the minority population when the dependent variables were the two continuous measures of child support, the magnitude of the coefficients was far too small to be noteworthy. Inexplicably, the direction of all three coefficients for the white population was actually positive, with the coefficient for receipt/nonreceipt approaching statistical significance (t-value = 1.71). This suggests that for the white population only, the passing of time might actually increase the chances of child support being paid by an originally reluctant father. However, when the dependent variables were total and average child support the coefficients were so small that they didn't even approach statistical significance. Thus there is only the scantiest evidence in support of the notion that low or nonexistent child support is a short-term, rather than a long-term, phenomenon.

As we previously discussed, the fact of remarriage on the part of the female head produced large negative coefficients with statistically significant t-values for all three dependent variables when tested with the white sample population. This is possibly because of judicial bias, as suggested earlier in this chapter, or because the former spouse withholds or reduces child support when the female head remarries for reasons which have nothing to do with the income of the new husband. The best explanation, we thought originally, lay in the fact that the Michigan Survey questionnaire is worded in such a way that child support and alimony are reported as one entity. Consequently, the decrement in "child support" which occurs at remarriage of the female head would be attributable to a stipulation in a divorce decree which abolishes alimony in the event of remarriage. However, if this had been the entire explanation for the reduction, there would have been no significant impact upon our dummy dependent variable—receipt/nonreceipt—as presumably the child support portion of the support payment could continue. Consequently, we rejected the "faulty measure" explanation. Whatever the reasons, remarriage accounted for a $684 decrement in the average child support payment for this group.

For minorities, however, the relationship between female head's remarriage and child support was clearly not as strong. The signs of the coefficients when the dependent variables were receipt/nonreceipt and total support were negative, as expected, but the magnitudes of both were considerably smaller than the comparable coefficients for whites—one tenth the size, to be precise. Thus, in terms of both the size and direction of the coefficients, remarriage of the minority female head probably does not have the significant impact upon child support that it does for whites, but the total picture does not allow us to reject the null hypothesis of lack of relationship between the two, either.

It will also be recalled that for the white sample population, the remarriage of the absent father actually had the effect of significantly increasing the amount of support he would contribute to his former family, even while controlling for his current wife's income. In terms of the minority sample population, however, a result emerged which was quite opposite that for the white population. The coefficients, though of lesser magnitude than those for whites, were negative for all three regression equations. When the dependent variable was total amount of support, the father's remarriage coefficient indicates a decrease of $344.25 ($t=1.31$). Apparently, for our minority sample population remarriage and the subsequent decrement in support suggests an attempt to sever previous relationships and their concomitant responsibilities— whether unilaterally, bilaterally, or at the insistence of the current wife we are not able to ascertain.

For neither the white nor the minority populations were the education of the absent spouse or the female head useful in predicting whether or not any child support was contributed. However, for whites both persons' educational attainment coefficients were positive when the dependent variables were average and total support, with t-values of 1.18 and 1.59 respectively for the absent fathers. There was an exception. A model containing squared values for the income and education measures for the white, minority, and combined populations was tested in the belief that relationships with the dependent variables would be evidenced. What was discovered by this effort was that a significant decline in child support does occur at higher levels of the father's education, but no similar relationships exist with the other variables. This was true only for the combined sample when the dependent variable was average per child amount of child support, however. On the other hand, for the minority population the education of the two parties had a much lesser impact upon average and total child support in terms of the magnitude of the coefficients, but, more interestingly, the direction of the coefficients differed from one another. With both dependent variables the absent father's coefficients were negative, while those for the female head were positive. Unlike the results for the white population, which susggested that increasing levels of educational attainment for both parties foster higher support, the results for the minority population suggest that higher levels of educational attainment for the absent father tend to depress child support, while higher levels of educational attainment for the female head may help, very slightly, to increase it. These results were so weak, however, that we have little confidence in them except in that they are suggestive of patterns that might bear further scrutiny. We thus have little evidence to support our view that the educational system helps to impart a sense of responsibility to the general population which might be manifested in seeking and receiving child support, on the part of the female head, and paying child support more often and at higher levels, on the part of the absent father.

Although none of the occupational categories for the female heads proved to have any impact upon receipt or levels of support, there did appear to be one trend that might warrant further investigation. Specifically, the coefficients for the white women's occupations were always positive but had an irregular magnitude pattern. Those for minority women, on the other hand, were irregular in terms of both the magnitude and the direction of the coefficients. Apparently the type of job a woman holds, all other things being equal, has little effect upon support payments she might receive.

Similarly, the coefficients for both white and minority female heads' education variables were consistently positive, but so small as to render them meaningless. These results and those for occupation suggest that a woman's ability to support herself, irrespective of current earnings, has little to do with whether or not she receives support, or if so in what amounts.

The coefficients for the occupation variables for the absent fathers were usually larger than those of the female heads and, as previously noted, were occasionally significant for the minority population, but in a negative direction. Similarly, the signs for the education coefficients were negative for the minority population, though the size of the coefficients was so small as to make conclusions impossible. The coefficient for white absent fathers' education was positive and large enough, however, to conclude that the extent of a father's education may have a slight impact upon the amount of support he pays controlling for all other factors.

Contrary to expectations, in every instance the coefficients for non-South (recall that this variable refers to the region in which the female-headed family lived, not to that of the absent father), bore negative signs indicating a pattern of lower and less frequent child support for those living in the West, North, and North Central regions. This was true for both the white and minority sample populations, and the magnitude of the coefficients, though not sizable, was almost identical for the two populations when the dependent variables were receipt/nonreceipt and total support. When the dependent variable was average support, however, the magnitude of the coefficient for the minority population remained small, while that for the white population increased substantially, indicating a reduction of $221 per child for those living outside the South. So not only do we have no evidence in support of our predicted regional effect, but in all instances the opposite effects were observed, one of which was statistically significant ($t=1.93$). Although this is contrary to our initial prediction, which was based upon the popular image of southern culture as being essentially white-male centered, our actual results either belie that image or may mean that social pressures to pay support are stronger in the South and might encourage the economic protection of one's children to a greater extent than elsewhere in the country.

The welfare status of the female head and the sum of the cash value of welfare and food stamps turned out to be insignificant as predictors of any of our dependent variables for either population. However, it should be noted that the signs of the coefficients were always in the predicted directions (positive for welfare status and negative for total amount of transfers), and often the *t*-values exceeded one. This suggests that a female head's participation in the AFDC program may actually increase her chances of getting child support, probably by gaining her access to free or reduced-cost legal services and, at the same time, reduce the amount of welfare she receives.

The illegitimate status of the child(ren) for whom child support was expected was quite surprisingly useless as a predictor of any of the dependent variables for either population. Not only were the *t*-values very small, but the signs of the coefficients went in both directions, depending upon the dependent variable being used. What this could mean is that, all other things being equal, whether or not a child is legitimate appears to have no bearing on whether he or she receives child support or how much is received from the absent father. It will be recalled, however, that when we created this variable we were lenient in our assumption of legitimacy (see page 43) and as a consequence very likely underestimated illegitimacy. It is quite possible also that never-married mothers might report their marital status as separated or divorced because of cultural tradition or fear of social embarrassment. Any or all of these could contribute to our finding of no discernible effect of illegitimate status upon child support payments. This question certainly requires further investigation.

Number of children eligible for support had the predictable effect in terms of results for both populations. That is, when the dependent variable was total amount of child support, the coefficient bore a positive sign and indicated that child support increased with each additional eligible child by approximately $152 for the white population and $16 for the minority population. On the other hand, when the dependent variable was average (per child) support, the coefficients bore negative signs for both populations, indicating that an additional child in a family eligible for child support had the effect of lowering the average amount each would receive. Again, this was in the direction predicted. Although the *t*-values of the coefficients for the minority population were less significant than those for the white population, we still have confidence that each population behaves in a similar fashion vis-à-vis child support and the number of children to be supported in a manner consistent with a notion of economies of scale.

The age of the youngest child at the time a couple splits appears to have no predictive value whatsoever for either population. No pattern could be discerned in terms of either the magnitude or the direction of the coefficients. This is not too surprising in light of the number of possible reasons why children of any age might be viewed as being more "costly" than children of any other age. That is, infants and toddlers may be more costly because of greater day-care expenses and medical needs, children of school age because of greater clothing and after-school-care costs, and adolescents because of increased nutritional requirements.

It was surprising to find that the number of children in the current family unit of the absent father had no negative impact upon any of the dependent variables for either population. In spite of the fact that a change in circumstances, which often includes the acquisition of new responsibilities, is legal justification for an absent father seeking modification or defending lower child support payments, we found no indication that, independent of all other measured factors, this one had the expected impact.

Findings for the Combined Population

Although we feel strongly that more is to be gained by testing our model on white and minority populations, as previously stated, the results produced when the sample size was increased by combining the two populations warrant our brief attention.

As expected, when the subsample populations were combined and the model was tested with the three dependent variables, all of the independent variables that were insignificant determinants of one or more of our dependent variables for either the white or the minority population were also insignificant determinants when these populations were combined. There was only one instance in which an independent variable that previously had not been statistically significant became so with the combined subsample. (This variable was the occupation dummy for unskilled laborer or service worker, the coefficient for which was positive and defies interpretation, especially in the absence of any discernible pattern in both the magnitude and direction of all of the absent father occupation coefficients.)

The qualitative and the quantitative differences between the results for the white and minority populations, when they occurred, we feel were important enough not to have been overlooked by combining the two sample populations. Though in general the directions of the coefficients were usually the same for both whites and minorities, the exceptions to this were rare and should not have been overlooked. Of major interest, however, is the fact that the magnitude of the coefficients differed substantially from one population to the other. Thus we feel that our original decision to test the model on the separate populations has been justified. Too much insight into the nature and the strength of the dynamics operating in the white and minority populations would have been lost by combining the two.

Summary of Findings

It appears that our model for the determinants of child support fits better when tested on the white subsample population. Not only is more of the variance in all three dependent variables explained by the model when it is tested on the white population, but the variables have greater statistical significance, suggesting that the determinants of child support for this population are more readily discernible, are more consistent with common knowledge or suppositions held by the general public, and have more impact than within the minority population. For this latter group, it is apparent that more of what determines payment and levels of child support lies outside the purview of this model.

On the other hand, what is suggested for both groups by the model is useful and interesting. For minorities, the most highly significant predictors of child support are the residence, income, and occupation of the absent father. These are all "supply-side" variables that are highly indicative of a voluntary quality of the child support phenomenon. Part of this result could be the consequence of the relative infrequency with which minorities seek mediation of the courts for resolution of interpersonal conflicts. A failure to make use of the legal system, the function of which is to resolve conflicts which arise between the demand and supply sides of the child support issue, could result in a child support payment system which would allow most, if not all, of the discretion to lie with the absent father. The extent of this discretion could be the cause of the apparent anomaly reported earlier, whereby minority men who held clerical or sales positions contributed more support than those who held professional or managerial occupations, who were less likely to be contributing any support at all.

Lastly, for the minority population the significance of the residence of the absent father as a determinant of support payments and levels may again reflect the discretion of the supplier of support, in that ease of visitation might promote interest in the child which in turn encourages more frequent and higher payments.

In terms of the white population, the direction and magnitude of the coefficients for the absent father's income, his current wife's income, the remarriage of the female head, the absent father's remarriage, and his retention in the sample after the split again are highly suggestive of "supply-side" dominance of our predictive model. It has been suggested that the drop in child support which is attributable to the remarriage of the female head really reflects her diminished need for it and is thus a "demand-side" variable. The author disagrees with this position because, first of all, the study controlled for the effect of the stepfather's income, for which there was no independent effect. Second, given the low levels of child support which were found to be the norm, and the low earnings of the female heads in our subsample, it seems clear that subsequent husbands are bearing a very large share of the costs of these stepchildren. It is quite unlikely, to the author, that a significant portion of them have voluntarily chosen to do so or are economically able to do so. They are likely providing most of their stepchildren's support because they have no other choice.

The number of children who are eligible for child support in a family unit may be the only independent variable which measures need, or the demand side. It will be recalled that this was a significant determinant of both total and average support levels for the white subsample population, and produced coefficients in the predicted directions for the minority sample population also.

The regional variable, which indicated an increase in all three measures of support when the mother and children lived in the South as opposed to the North, North Central, or West, could reflect a judiciary bias of southern courts that places more emphasis on the economic needs of children than do nonsouthern courts. On the other hand, to the extent that this coefficient reflects a regional difference in the attitudes of the absent fathers—that is, southern fathers value their children more, or they may value complying with the law or social expectations more, than nonsouthern fathers—then it shifts to the "supply" side of the equation.[1,2]

Given that we wish the redistribution of resources within these former families to be accomplished in a manner that balances the needs of the children's family unit with the ability to pay manifested by that of the absent father, policy questions should be directed at the causes of and social solutions for these obstacles and distortions in the child support enforcement system—distortions that result in a system which is very suggestive of a voluntary, highly discretionary pattern of child support payment.

In the chapters that follow, we will incorporate the insights we have gained from testing our model in some suggestions for future research, policy, and programmatic recommendations.

Notes

1. Max Rheinstein, *Marriage Stability, Divorce, and the Law,* The University of Chicago Press: Chicago, 1972, p. 380.

2. Kenneth R. White and R. Thomas Stone, Jr., "A Study of Alimony and Child Support Rulings with Some Recommendations," *Family Law Quarterly,* Vol. X, No. 1: Spring 1976, p. 83.

3. William Goode, *Women in Divorce,* The Free Press: New York, 1956, pp. 221-227.

4. "Successful enforcement" refers to the likelihood that public efforts to collect support will result in actual collections, and in no way reflects the extent to which the support collected compares with the required or adjudicated support or the absent father's ability to pay.

5. *Detailed Summary of Findings: Absent Parent Child Support Cost-Benefit Analysis,* Arthur Young and Company, prepared under contract No. SRS-7456, for Social and Rehabilitation Service, Department of Health, Education and Welfare: 1975, pp. 44-46, 62-64.

6. Unpublished results used with permission of author. Feb. 1978.

7. Michael McFadden, *Bachelor Fatherhood,* Ace Books: New York, p. 22, and Susan R. Sewell, *Compliance with Child Support Obligations,* unpublished paper prepared in partial fulfillment of requirements for LL.B. degree, University of Texas Law School: Spring 1976, p. 16.

8. Unless otherwise noted, all of the variables were measured in 1975.

9. *Detailed Summary of Findings,* op. cit., p. 63.

10. Heather L. Ross and Isabel V. Sawhill, *Time of Transition: The Growth of Families Headed by Women,* the Urban Institute: Washington, D.C., 1975, p. 51.

11. Martin R. Levy and Elaine C. Duncan, "The Impact of Roe Versus Wade on Paternal Support Statutes: A Constitutional Analysis," *Family Law Quarterly,* Vol. X, No. 3: Fall 1976, p. 189.

12. Shortly following the completion of this research, a working paper was sent to the author by Isabel Sawhill, a senior research staff member at the Urban Institute, in which the preliminary results of her work in the area of child support-alimony payment performance were reported. When the final results are available they will add a great deal to the knowledge we now have. Nevertheless, the conclusion one can draw from her preliminary work is strikingly similar to our own, to wit, "supply-side" variables dominated her predictive model of child support payment performance, as did those in our model. See Carol Adair Jones, Nancy M. Gordon, and Isabel Sawhill, *Child Support Payments in the United States,* Working Paper 992-03, The Urban Institute: Washington, D.C., October 1, 1976, pp. 90-109.

4

How Much Child Support Can Fathers Afford?

Introduction

The topic of this chapter—the ability of the absent father to pay child support—is perhaps the most controversial of all those related to the enforcement issue. Few would argue that a child has the right to the support of both parents and, similarly, few would argue that the public has some responsibility for enforcing that right. One might encounter debate as to the proper mechanism or system for enforcing the child's right or the parental obligation and the extent to which coercion should be employed, but these are issues reserved for later discussion. For the present time we shall confine our discussion to the topic of ability to pay.

In this regard, it is interesting to note that a child's right to support by his or her father does not, either by statute or in practice, take priority over the father's ability to provide that support. Thus it is the surplus—the amount in excess of his current needs—which is the implicit ceiling on the measure of ability to pay. Unfortunately, the civil codes of the states do not provide definitions or guidelines for specifying ability to pay, nor have the courts been eager to adopt a uniform definition because of the strictly defended tradition of judicial autonomy and discretion in the matter of setting support payments.[1] In spite of laws in most states that grant a child the right to claim support based upon the father's ability to pay—ensuring, supposedly, a life-style equivalent to that which would have been enjoyed prior to the divorce or had no divorce occurred[2]—these laws are rarely found to operate in practice, largely because of the absence of a standard measure of ability to pay and the strength of the ethos which protects the prerogative of the court to determine ability to pay on a case-by-case basis.[3] Occasionally, judges have themselves been denied by statute the right to impose standards or formulas, based upon a single measure of ability to pay, which would have assured more equity between families.[4] Thus from within both the judicial and the legislative arenas, a maximum amount of discretion has been preserved with which to define ability to pay.

The value of preserving discretion in the definition of ability to pay is that extenuating or unusual circumstances in the lives of any or all parties can be accommodated. A standard definition of ability to pay might tend to result in an inflexible formula that could impose undue hardship on one group of persons, or systematically favor another group. The relative value of these arguments will be discussed in later chapters.

We have learned from the empirical analysis in chapter 3 which factors appear to explain levels of child support. From this analysis, we have suggested that factors which reflect a father's willingness to pay support and the extent of his economic resources appear to explain vastly more of the variance in child support than does the economic need or desire for support (for which there is no really adequate measure) on the part of the child support-dependent family. What we do not yet know, however, is how well off each side of the former family is, relative to the other. In addition, we do not know how many more fathers are able to pay support than are presently doing so and, among those who are paying, how much more could be paid. Furthermore, we do not know the extent to which any additional support would improve the economic well-being of those female-headed families who would be its recipients. In other words, using a maximum measure of the absent father's ability to pay child support, vis-à-vis the dependent family's need for it, what amount of money could be realized and what impact would it have upon the relative economic well-being of the children's family unit?

Before addressing these questions directly, it will be useful to see what support payments presently look like in relation to the income of the absent father.

Using data from our Michigan Survey subsample as used in chapters 2 and 3, Table 4-1 illustrates the relationships between child support and the absent father's income in 1974. As can readily be seen, even when gross taxable income exceeded $15,000 per year, the proportion of absent fathers who paid support was only two-thirds. Recall that the 1975 data are based upon circumstances in 1974. Even at this upper income level, the mean child support payment for the two thirds who were paying was just $2,274, which was only slightly more than half of the poverty level for a family of three in 1974. See Table A-13 in the Appendix for Social Security Administration poverty levels by family size. (What we cannot see, however, and what we have no way of knowing given the limitations of our data set, is what proportion of these female heads of households actually want to receive financial assistance from the fathers of their children. For the purposes of this analysis we will assume that, all other things being equal, most would prefer this kind of help to none at all.) In addition, child support, in the event it was being paid at all, appeared to be highly regressive, with lower-income fathers paying a much larger percentage of their incomes in child support than did higher-income fathers.

Thus in spite of the fact that most states' civil codes implicitly suggest that support be progressive, with higher-income fathers paying support in amounts which represent larger percentages of their incomes, the opposite appears to be the case. At least some of the responsibility for this distortion might lie with attorneys and the courts. Although there is some empirical evidence that judges strive for progressivity[5] and that attorneys who practice family law find progressivity both reasonable and normatively desirable,[6] several factors might

Table 4-1
Child Support and the Income of the Absent Father in 1975

Income of Absent Father	Number of Fathers	Number Paying Support	Percent Paying Support	Mean Support (of those paying)	Mean Support (including those not paying)	Mean Child Support as a Percentage of Absent Father's Income
Family Splits						
$0-1,500	18	3	17	$ 367	$ 61	25
1,501-3,000	8	2	25	1,000	250	33
3,001-5,000	21	3	14	700	100	14
5,001-7,500	38	8	21	888	187	12
7,501-10,000	30	6	20	1,283	257	13
10,001-15,000	43	21	49	1,505	735	10
15,001	35	23	66	2,274	1,494	11
Income Unknown (Female heads, husbands never in sample)	385	54	14	1,335	187	–
Total	578	120	(48 Family Splits)	1,467	304	Mean for Family Splits only $539

combine to produce a result that is exactly contrary to that intended. First, many judges increase support with the number of children for whom it is intended. If low-income families have more children than do their more prosperous counterparts, this practice could contribute to apparent regressivity when support is measured as a percentage of a father's income. Second, most judges may use net income, instead of gross income, as the basis for setting child support.[7] This practice would tend to favor high-income fathers whose "paper" tax liability may be vastly different from the actual economic benefits they enjoy. Finally, there is a prevailing belief that the division of income between father and child must take into consideration the right of a father to a life-style consistent with his income, and the right to begin a new family if he wishes.[8] To the extent that higher-income fathers with fewer child support-dependent children are viewed as deserving a greater measure of the right to begin a new life than are lower-income fathers with larger numbers of dependents, regressivity could result.

As for ceilings on support, in terms of the payments as a percentage of father's income, our Table 4-1 shows it to be 33 percent. Interestingly enough, this turns out to be precisely the maximum amount suggested by both *The Family Law Reporter,* a journal of the Bureau of National Affairs, Inc.,[9] and a family court judge in an article referred to earlier.[10] The empirical findings of John J. Sampson of the University of Texas Law School suggest that the practice of imposing a ceiling on child support closely follows the normative standards proposed by this judge and the Bureau of National Affairs. Professor Sampson found that average child support awards in Texas virtually never exceeded 37 percent of an absent father's *net* income. Texas averages also took account of the number of children who were to be the child support recipients, which created an anomaly whereby a father with a net monthly income of $410 paid $150 for the support of five children, subjecting him to a 37 percent implicit tax rate on his earnings, while a father with a net income of $1,433 paid an average of $277, which was only 19 percent of his income, in support for one child.[11] This same pattern can be observed in most normative standard tables that try to take account of numbers of support-dependent children. However, Sampson was quick to point out that the term "average" as used to describe the support awards could be very misleading as the amount of variance in support orders, both between counties and within counties, was large enough to be termed by him, in part at least, "arbitrary" and "capricious."[12] Sampson's findings appear to be similar to those of another researcher, whose conclusions were based upon questionnaire responses from 86 percent of the family court judges in Illinois. Only one judge was able to recall an instance in which adjudicated support reached 50 percent of an absent father's income. Most of the judges surveyed reported the concept of average support to be meaningless owing to the vast number of factors which must be taken into consideration with each case.[13]

While the earned income of the absent father, whether gross or net of federal and state taxes, certainly appears to be the most prevalent measure of ability to pay, other factors are reported to enter into the court's estimation. These include the value of assets held or transferred by the absent father, benefits in kind he might be receiving,[14] needs of a current family,[15] employment-related expenses, and, interestingly enough, the likelihood that the absent father would comply with the support order. One judge, in fact, found the compliance issue to be of such concern as to preclude his awarding support which was in excess of public assistance levels, asserting that fathers required to pay amounts in excess of welfare benefit levels simply would not do so.[16]

Among the factors which researchers have found to influence judicial assessment of the support-dependent family's need were the number of children and their ages, the earning capacity of the custodial parent, the health status of all the principals, assets and financial obligations such as mortgage payments, and finally, the standard of living which the children had enjoyed prior to the divorce.[17]

Although there are no major conflicts between our empirical findings as to the determinants of levels of support (reported in chapter 3), the empirical findings of others as to levels of support (in absolute terms and as a percentage of the absent father's income), and the normative statements as to what should constitute a measure of ability to pay, there is an obvious dearth of discussion of and empirical inquiry into the extent to which payment levels meet, or should meet, the needs of a dependent family. In other words, though some authors have admonished attorneys and judges to consider the needs of the dependent family when adjudicating support, neither the civil code, the common law, or the empirical results suggest that for the population as a whole, the needs of the support-dependent family are given consideration at least equal to that of the absent father's ability to pay.

The exception to this occurs when the support-dependent family seeks public assistance. At this point, great emphasis is placed upon the needs of the dependent family, and it is precisely when this shift in emphasis occurs that the separation between the private and the public systems of child support enforcement emerges. This separation is made clear by the respective focuses in the literature from the disciplines of law and social welfare. In that of the former, the emphasis is upon the ability of the absent father to pay support, while that of the latter focuses upon the inadequacy of that support in terms of the needs of the dependent family.[18] The analysis which follows in this chapter may be the first attempt to explore simultaneously the question of the extent to which actual child support reflects the availability of resources in control of the absent father, and the needs and resources of the support-dependent family. In other words, we will get a more complete picture of the extent of resources which might be taken into account when ascertaining the amount of support which the father could contribute relative to the amount which the children require.

In order to address this question, we will explore the impact, in terms of the relative economic positions of the absent father and the female-headed family, of child support payments based upon measures of ability to pay in relation to need.

The Data

For the remainder of this chapter, we have chosen to use only the family splits from our Michigan subsample. When possible, formerly married couples were rematched so that information pertaining to each person would be appropriately cross-referenced. In the event that an absent father became a nonrespondent following the split, we imputed marital status and current wives' data for a randomly selected 35 percent, because this percentage was identical to that of the absent fathers who were retained in the survey after a split and who subsequently remarried. The remaining 65 percent of the nonrespondent absent fathers were treated as though they had not remarried. Thus there were no current wives' earnings, no subsequent children, and the SSA poverty level was for one person living alone. Income measures for the entire group of nonrespondent fathers was inflated, as in chapter 3, by the appropriate rate from the last year each was interviewed.

It is likely that these latter manipulations have added to the bias which has been inherent in the "family splits" subsample all along. That is, the family splits have evidenced characteristics representative of socioeconomic status higher than those of the other two subsample groupings, especially those family splits for whom data were available from both parties for the years after the split. It appears, though, that the female-headed families for which absent fathers became nonrespondents are more similar to the rest of the subsample members than are the families for which absent fathers were retained after the split. Thus, by imputing the demographic characteristics of retained absent fathers to those who disappeared from the sample, we have added to the nonrepresentativeness of our subsample. The overall effect of this is that our results are most certainly overestimates of the ability of these absent fathers to pay support, though precisely to what extent cannot be ascertained.

The Income-Poverty Ratio and Ability to Pay Support

First, we begin by comparing the income-poverty ratios,[19] based upon earned income, of the absent father and the household which contains his dependent children by a former union. For the purpose of the analyses in this chapter, only subsample members whose husbands were sample members at some point during the survey years ("family splits") will be used, as we require precise data on absent fathers which are not available for those who were female heads at the onset of the study in 1968, or for those who joined our subsample as female heads and whose husbands had never been heads of sample families. Thus:

Income ÷ Social Security Administration poverty level for family size

= Family income-poverty ratio

Excluding transfer payments from our measure of income, a comparison of the income-poverty ratios of the absent fathers with those of the dependent family gives us a picture of relative well-being based upon income-generating behavior, family size, and location. Nontransfer, nonearned income from assets, such as stocks and interest on savings accounts, are included in this measure. Public transfers, such as AFDC, are not included in the measure of personal income as they are income-conditioned and thus out of sequence for present purposes, since child support is treated as other unearned income in figuring AFDC eligibility and payment levels. In both cases, the income and needs of current spouses, if any, as well as the needs of children acquired with or born to those subsequent unions, are included in the numerator and the denominator, respectively.

Table 4-2 presents the distributions of absent father and female head income-poverty ratios side by side, for purposes of comparison. It will be noted that 19 percent of the dependent families in our subsample have income-poverty

Table 4-2
Distribution of Income-Poverty Ratios for Absent Fathers and Households Containing the Dependent Children in 1974[a]

| | | Frequency | | Percentage in Subsample | |
| | | Dependent | Absent | Dependent | Absent |
Class	Class Intervals	Households	Fathers	Households	Fathers
1	0 -0.49	350,000	42,500	15.32	1.86
2	0.5-0.99	76,000	26,500	3.33	1.16
3	1.0-1.49	270,000	30,000	11.82	1.31
4	1.5-1.99	210,000	22,500	9.22	.99
5	2.0-2.49	199,500	63,500	8.73	2.78
6	2.5-100	1,178,000	2,099,000	51.58	91.90

[a]This table and those that follow in this chapter are based upon the Michigan Survey weighted subsample "family splits" only. Because of the nature of the weighting procedure, the total number of observations in each table (2,284,000 here) may vary slightly due to rounding errors. However, proportions, means, and so forth will be consistent, as these rounding errors do not account for more than a one percent difference.

ratios less than unity, whereas only 3 percent of the absent fathers share this plight. An income-poverty ratio that is less than unity means that a family unit has earned income that is less than the SSA poverty level for its size and location. Because female heads from previously intact families ("family splits") were substantially better off by all measures of socioeconomic status than were their subsample counterparts (see Table A-1 in Appendix), it is not surprising that only 19 percent of them had income-poverty ratios less than unity compared with the higher proportion reported in chapter 2 for the overall subsample. Another factor which diminishes the proportion who are poor is our inclusion of remarried women, who were excluded from the analysis in chapter 2 and whose husbands' incomes as well as needs were included in the ratio. It will be recalled that remarriage was found by Ross and Sawhill to be the single greatest factor in the reduction in the incidence of poverty for female-headed families.

Table 4-2, however, does not allow us to see how pairs of former spouses' ratios are distributed. That is, if we subtract the income-poverty ratio of each dependent family from that of the absent father, what will the distribution of those net figures look like? Table 4-3 yields such a distribution, and it is apparent that the overwhelming majority of absent spouses (86 percent) were

Table 4-3
Distribution of Comparative Income-Poverty Ratios[a]

Class	Difference Intervals	Frequency	Percentage of Subsample Population
1	−100 to −2.5	132,000	5.75
2	−2.49 to −2.0	27,500	1.20
3	−1.99 to −1.5	74,500	3.25
4	−1.49 to −1.0	19,000	.83
5	−0.99 to −0.5	2,000	.09
6	−0.49 to 0	66,000	2.88
7	0.01 to 0.49	128,000	5.58
8	0.50 to 0.99	80,500	3.51
9	1.0 to 1.49	149,000	6.49
10	1.5 to 1.99	140,000	6.10
11	2.0 to 2.49	153,500	6.69
12	2.5 to 100	1,322,500	57.64

[a]From the absent father's income-poverty ratio we subtracted that of the dependent household. Difference intervals preceded by minus signs indicate dependent households which were better off than those of the absent father (classes 1 through 5). Classes 6 and 7 indicate that both are about the same in terms of "well-offness," and those from 8 up indicate increasing degrees of imbalance favoring the households of the absent fathers. Total number of observations is 2,294,500.

better off than their former wives and children and over 64 percent had income-poverty ratios which were two or more times greater than those of their former wives and children.

An obvious limitation of the above analysis is that although we have been able to identify those dependent families with income "deficits," and the absent fathers with "surplus" income, we still need to determine how far that surplus could go toward closing the income gap between the two families. The following attempts to do this.

In determining how far the resources of the absent father might go toward closing the income gap between him and his former family, it is clear that we cannot assume that all of the surplus which is above and beyond his current needs is available. In so doing, an imbalance that would favor the female-headed family could be created. We are striving here for balance between the two families, and not a reversal of the imbalanced situation. Thus it is necessary to impose two reasonable constraints upon the sum which we take from the absent father in our efforts to achieve balance. These constraints are (1) that we will not reduce an absent father's income-poverty ratio to a point less than unity, and (2) that we will not reduce his ratio to a point less than that of the children and their mother. The procedure for arriving at an approximate estimate of the amount required to equalize income-poverty ratios thus becomes: If his income-poverty ratio is less than unity, or her income-poverty ratio is greater than his, no money is assumed to be available for child support. However, in the event a transfer is in order, the amount of that transfer is equal to

$$\frac{(Y_{af} - PL_{af}) - (Y_{df} - PL_{df})}{2}$$

where

Y_{af} and Y_{df} = the pretransfer income of the absent father and dependent family, respectively, and

PL_{af} and PL_{df} = the SSA poverty levels by family size for the absent father and dependent family, respectively.

We are now in a position to answer the following questions:

1. What could the average family transfer be under these conditions?
2. What proportion of the female-headed families would still have income-poverty ratios less than unity? (In other words, how many would still be poor by SSA standards? Nineteen percent of our subsample have income-poverty ratios less than unity under the present system, it will be recalled.)
3. Of these dependent families, which ones still have deficits and how much

money would be required, in total and on the average, to raise them to the poverty threshold?

4. How do the above answers compare with answers based upon the actual child support payments being made as a consequence of the present system?

The preliminary answers turn out to be rather surprising. For this group of 193 family splits, the average child support payment in 1974 was only $539. "Average child support" received includes the majority who received no child support whatsoever in 1974. However, the mean expected child support turns out to be almost $3,566 per year, a difference of about $3,027! Recall that this figure includes income and needs of both the absent father and his former wife, in addition to those of their current spouses and all children in their present family units.

Now as our more narrow concern lies with the potential impact of child support upon the poor and the near-poor dependent family, it is helpful to disaggregate our data so that we can focus our attention upon these populations. Table 4-4 divides the sample population of families into three classes based upon income-poverty status. The first class is made up of those who are clearly poor—those whose earnings alone are insufficient to raise them above the poverty threshold. ("Class" is determined on the basis of pretransfer income of the female head's family unit, not that of the absent father.) Class 2 are those whose income-poverty ratios place them close enough to the poverty level to render them "at risk" for poverty status. That is, a nonfarm family of four with an income of about $8,000 per year may be over $3,000 away from officially designated poverty status, but would be very vulnerable to such if it were to experience a prolonged illness of the major breadwinner, for instance. Class 3 includes those for whom poverty is not as likely to pose such an imminent threat. In order to maximize the number of useful observations for the purposes of this analysis, we included absent fathers who had disappeared from the survey sample after the family split. By including this group, we increased our number of observations and thus the usefulness of the data. However, because of the fact that important information pertaining to the absent father's current family status, the income status of a current wife, if any, and so forth was missing, we imputed values for these characteristics to them based upon the means for the absent fathers who were retained in the survey population. To the extent that the values in question were comparable for the retained and nonrespondent absent fathers, we have enhanced the value of our findings. Had we not included the nonrespondent absent fathers, our subsample size would have been so small within some classes as to render our averages meaningless.

It is surprising to find that under our measure of ability to pay based upon earned income, for Class 1 an average of $4,062 is available from which support for the dependent family could derive. We find that for this group of pretransfer poor families, an average of only $287 would additionally be required in order

Table 4-4
Summary of Income-Poverty Status After Child Support Payments

Class	Number	Y/PL of Female-Headed Household	Actual Child Support Received in 1974	Y/PL Deficit After Actual Child Support	Expected Child Support if Income-Poverty Ratios were Equalized	Y/PL Deficit After Expected Child Support
1 (Poor)	86	0–.99	$292.73	$2,964.08	$4,062.55	$286.72 (for 66 still poor)
2 ("At Risk")	40	1.00–2.00	517.15	—	2,265.55	—
3 (Nonpoor)	67	2.01–	867.67	—	3,705.69	—
Total	193		538.84 (mean)		3,565.79 (mean)	

Note: Y/PL_{SSA} = Income-Poverty ratio as described in Chapter 4. That is, the total, non-transfer income of an individual is divided by the appropriate Social Security Administration poverty level to yield a measure of relative economic well-being.

to make those who are still poor after the expected support payments nonpoor. The fact that any deficit remains after such a large assumed child support payment is likely the result of a large number of children in the home of a female head with very low earnings. This suggests that increased child support enforcement efforts toward extracting a maximum amount of child support from absent fathers could succeed in significantly reducing the extent of economic dependence of female-headed families, and comes close to abolishing poverty altogether.

As we look at Class 2, those whom we might conclude are "at risk" in terms of poverty—those who would likely be poor if child support and/or earnings dropped—we find that the amount of expected child support shrinks considerably (to $2,266), most likely because of fewer children in the household of a female head and/or her greater earnings. It is from this group that a great deal of AFDC savings might come, by preventing through child support collection and dispersal economic dependence upon the public sector.

A similar analysis can be applied to Class 3 families who, obviously, are further removed from poverty levels, apparently more through their own income-generating behavior (and/or that of their current husbands) than through high child support payments, though the latter apparently contribute to their greater economic well-being. Though Class 3 families are not as precariously placed regarding the poverty threshold, we should still be concerned, for reasons of equity, with the magnitude of the differential between actual child support payments and the potential amount available when we use income as a measure of absent father's ability to pay. A very interesting result of this analysis is that there is less difference between the transfers needed to approximate equalization of income-poverty ratios for female heads in Class 1 and those in Class 3 ($4,062 and $3,706 respectively) than one might expect. Most likely this is due principally to the higher earnings of the Class 3 female heads (and/or current husband), rather than to relatively equal resources of Class 1 and Class 3 absent fathers. This result may also suggest, given this measure of ability to pay, that as a female head's own income-generating resources are enhanced, the amount of money required to make her as well-off as the absent spouse declines.

Looking at Table 4-5, which contains the same analysis as Table 4-4 but only for those who receive public transfers (AFDC, food stamps, and emergency assistance), we find, not surprisingly, that actual child support payments at all levels are much lower than they were for the group as a whole (Table 4-4), which has probably contributed to their eligibility for public transfers in the first place. For Class 1, the income-poverty deficit after actual child support payments is slightly larger than it was in Table 4-4, reflecting the lower support payments and possibly slightly larger family size. Similarly, and again not surprisingly, the expected child support has diminished considerably, probably owing to decreased earnings of this group of absent fathers and to a lesser extent higher earnings of female heads, which may be partly the consequence of work requirements for AFDC eligibility.

Table 4-5

Summary of Income-Poverty Status After Child Support Payments (For Only Those Who Received Public Transfers in 1974)[a]

Class	Number	Y/PL Female-Headed Household	Actual Child Support Received in 1974	Y/PL Deficit After Actual Child Support	Expected Child Support if Income-Poverty Ratios were Equalized	Y/PL Deficit After Expected Child Support
1	63	0– .99	$102.70	$3,425.67	$3,446.52	$382.44 (for 43 still poor)
2	13	1.00–2.00	289.23	–	1,580.08	–
3	3	2.01–	–	–	1,883.50	–
Total	79		129.49 (mean)		3,080.03 (mean)	

[a]Anyone with AFDC, other welfare, or food stamps with cash value greater than zero.

As we look at Classes 2 and 3, it becomes apparent that the earnings of these female heads and their current husbands, if any, may have contributed to their distance from the poverty threshold, and that the small amount of actual child support is probably due to very low ability to generate income relative to present needs on the part of the absent father, or else the expected child support figures would be larger. For those who are surprised to find persons receiving public transfers whose pretransfer incomes place them above SSA poverty levels, remember that some states are able to provide higher benefits than others and may need to do so because of particularly high costs of living in these areas. Also, note that 68 percent of this population have incomes below SSA poverty levels, while only 32 percent are above. Interestingly enough, for this population of public transfer recipients, the availability of resources which might be used to approximate the equalization of income-poverty ratios within these pairs of families actually is far greater for Class 1 female heads than for Class 2 or 3. This suggests that although the absent fathers of AFDC-dependent children may have fewer resources than other absent fathers, greater amounts of money are required from them, most likely because of larger numbers of children in the female-headed family, and far less earnings. At the time of the analyses reported here, we identified twenty absent fathers who were able or expected to pay no support, for either of the two reasons specified earlier—that they had incomes insufficient for meeting the needs of current families, or that former families were economically better off than they were. Every one of the former families of these twenty men were enumerated among the welfare-recipient group.

It should be apparent by now that this particular measure of ability to pay support, and the manifest need of the support-dependent family, is a highly dynamic one. That is, a change in family size or income on the part of either half of these former families will cause a change in the final figure—the amount which might be viewed as available or expected as child support.

The Welfare Ratio and Ability to Pay Support

It has been suggested by other researchers that income alone is not a measure of economic well-being that fully captures the economic status of a family.[21] Furthermore, if a family were to employ both its human and physical assets at their capacity, the picture of relative economic well-being that would emerge might be at odds with that which appears when income alone is used as the measure of economic well-being. As we discussed earlier in this chapter, some family courts have also tried to employ a similar concept. The literature from the field of family law occasionally makes normative or empirical statements to the effect that support is or should be based upon a concept of earnings capacity rather than actual earnings. Though this concept may be used to justify support judgments against a man even when he is temporarily unemployed,[22] it may also be used to justify lower awards to female heads of families whom the courts feel should be working,[23] or possibly to motivate them to seek employment. Nevertheless, the concept of earnings capacity as a measure of ability to pay support, vis-à-vis the need for it, is an important one, the consequences of which should be explored further.

We have chosen for present analytic purposes the Garfinkel-Haveman definition of earnings capacity, as the "net returns which a family would anticipate if it were to employ its human and physical assets at their capacity."[24] As such, it will be a function of measures of human capital such as: "*age,* taken to reflect job experience and training as well as the obsolescence of skills and physical and mental capacities with advanced years [disability due to advancing years is less likely in our subsample, as the variance in the age measures was narrow due to the requirement that there be minor children for whom support was to be expected]; *years of schooling,* to reflect the stock of human capital conveyed by education; *race,* to reflect labor market discrimination among blacks and whites; *marital status,* to reflect the higher incidence of physical and mental disabilities and other characteristics leading to lower labor productivity among single than married persons ["other characteristics" in this instance would also include the additional incentive to supply more labor on the part of the absent father who takes on subsequent family responsibility and, possibly, the reduced labor supply of a female head who remarries, which is consistent with what Garfinkel and Haveman found—that married women with children earn less than single women with children[25]]; *location,* to capture real productivity differences not captured by the human capital variables, and weeks worked and part-time, full-time employment status."[26] In addition, sex will be included in the measures of earnings capacity in order to capture labor market discrimination reflected in wage, salary, and occupational differentials based upon sex.

On the basis of the coefficients associated with the above variables, and the assumption that each adult in all of our family units worked at capacity, we estimated Gross Earnings Capacity (GEC) for every dependent family and absent father in our subsample.[27] (See Table A-22 in the Appendix for formula).

Finally, it is important that our estimate of earnings capacity be netted of the single greatest expense associated with the employment of all of the adults in a family unit—child-care costs. Accordingly, we subtracted from the estimate of Gross Earnings Capacity for each family unit $1,721 annually for each child five years old or less, and $429 annually for each child six to fourteen years of age, according to nationwide estimates of average day-care costs. These estimates, made in 1970, have been inflated to correspond with 1974 prices and thus be comparable to all of the other dollar measures in this work. Because of the enormous variance in child-care costs between geographic locations, these estimates are rough, at best.[28]

Thus, the estimate of the Net Earnings Capacity for each family unit is:

$$NEC_{fu} = GEC_{fu} - C_{cc}$$

where

GEC_{fu} = Gross Earnings Capacity estimate for the family unit

C_{cc} = The total costs of child care for the family unit.

Again, the current measure of economic well-being, in this case the estimate of Net Earnings Capacity, is placed in the numerator position, while the Social Security Administration poverty level, adjusted for family size, is placed in the denominator position, to give us a net welfare ratio, referred to hereinafter as the welfare ratio.

Thus,

$$WR_{fu} = \frac{NEC_{fu}}{PL_{ssa}}$$

An examination of the distribution of welfare ratios of absent fathers and those of dependent families, comparable to the income-poverty ratios in Table 4-2, indicates that the assumption of full-time employment to capacity on the part of all adults had the effect of almost totally eliminating all absent fathers from the ranks of the poor, but producing a reduction of only 9 percent for the dependent families which were headed by women (see Table A-14 in the

Appendix). This suggests for the most part that these women are already working at capacity outside the home.

The distribution of comparative welfare ratios (see Table A-15 in the Appendix) reduced some of the disparity which was found earlier when we subtracted the income-poverty ratios of dependent families from those of absent fathers. When economic well-being was measured by estimates of earnings capacity instead of earned income alone, far fewer women were found to be worse off than their former spouses, suggesting that for this subsample at least, welfare ratios of pairs of former spouses were, to a very small extent, more comparable than were their income-poverty ratios.

In spite of these subtle changes in relative economic well-being that appear when measures of earnings capacity are used rather than the more traditional measures of economic well-being based upon market earnings, we found that for the entire subsample population for family splits, an average annual amount of $2,934 could be assumed available for child support (see Table 4-6) when we employ our modified formula for equalizing welfare ratios, as follows:

$$\frac{(NEC_{af} - PL_{af}) - (NEC_{df} - PL_{df})}{2}$$

This is about $453 less than the $3,387 which we calculated would be available if we were to use actual earnings as a measure of economic well-being. Though not an enormous difference, it is certainly a significant one, and suggests that we might need to take a closer look at the consequences of using earnings capacity as a measure of economic well-being for purposes such as this. Therefore, we turn now to a determination of the differential amounts of child support we could expect when disaggregating into the poor, near-poor, and nonpoor populations, as we did earlier with our income-poverty ratio analysis.

Table 4-6
Summary of Welfare Ratio Status After Child Support Payments Using Earnings Capacity as a Measure of Economic Well-Being

Class	Number	Welfare Ratios of Female-Headed Households	Actual Chlid Support Received in 1974	Welfare Ratio Deficit After Actual Child Support	Expected Child Support to Equalize Welfare Ratios	Welfare Ratio Deficit After Expected Child Support
1	72	0– .99	$276.74	$2,517.58	$4,107.16	–
2	67	1.00–2.00	549.58	–	2,847.41	–
3	49	2.01–	846.74	–	1,326.63	–
Total	188		522.54 (mean)		2,933.49 (mean)	

A number of surprises emerge when we use earnings capacity as our basic measure of economic well-being for the absent father and female-headed households. First, the actual amounts of child support being paid, by welfare ratio class, are strikingly similar to those paid when female heads are classified by income-poverty ratios. Similarly, the proportion of female heads found in each class does not change dramatically with the manner in which economic well-being is measured. However, a startling decrement in expected child support occurs as the economic well-being of the female-headed family increases. A comparison with the figures in Table 4-4 indicates that for poor female heads, the expected child support from the absent father is almost identical when child support is based upon estimates of earnings capacity. This suggests that both absent fathers and female heads are most likely already employing the maximum amount of their human capital in the labor market, especially at low income levels. When the availability of resources which might be expected as child support and the need for it are based upon measures of earnings capacity, Class 2 (near-poor) dependent families can expect about $582 more than if they were based upon actual income. Class 3 families, on the other hand, can only expect $1,327, $2,379 *less* than that which would be based upon actual earnings! Precisely the same pattern, with little variation in the dollar amounts, is in evidence for the welfare-recipient population also (see Table 4-7). Apparently, then, when earnings capacity is used as the basic measure of economic well-being for both the subsample population as a whole and a population consisting only of welfare recipients, the amounts of child support required to approximate the equalization of economic well-being between absent fathers and female heads declines as their relative well-being improves. On the surface, this may appear to be regressive. The total evidence suggests, however, that because of a number of factors—larger family size among the poor, greater remarriage rates among nonpoor female heads, and so forth—both actual income and estimates of earnings capacity, when used as basic measures of ability to pay, suggest larger expected payments among the near-poor, and payments which are much larger than the payments for those further removed from poverty.

A firm note of caution about extrapolating from these results to the general population is in order. First, these calculations are based upon the subsample of "family splits"—families which were intact during at least one year of the Michigan Survey. It was necessary to use only the family splits because we needed absent-father attributes for our calculations, attributes which were not available in the event a subsample member was already a female head in 1968 or had been a subfamily member in an original sample family before setting up her own household. Thus we have excluded from this analysis two very important types of female heads that have been used for analytic purposes in our previous chapters—those who were female heads in the study's base year (who tended to be older women who had been separated or divorced longer than the others), and those who moved out of a sample-family household during one of

Table 4-7

Summary of Welfare Ratio Status After Child Support Payments Using Earnings Capacity as a Measure of Economic Well-Being (For Only Those Who Received Public Transfers in 1974)[a]

Class	Number	Welfare Ratios of Female-Headed Households	Actual Child Support Received in 1974	Welfare Ratio Deficit After Actual Child Support	Expected Child Support to Equalize Welfare Ratios	Welfare Ratio Deficit After Expected Child Support
1	49	0– .99	$143.16	$2,856.49	$4,202.61	–
2	26	1.00–2.00	108.31	–	2,133.22	–
3	3	2.01–	–	–	1,273.93	–
Total	78		126.04 (mean)		3,400.17 (mean)	

[a]Anyone with AFDC, other welfare, or food stamps with cash value greater than zero.

the survey years (who were usually unmarried, rather young mothers). Both of these types of female-head subsample members possess demographic characteristics which are more like those of the AFDC population than of the family splits. Thus our figures in this chapter, which are based upon the characteristics of family splits only, may represent an absolute ceiling on the availability of cash resources because the demographic characteristics of this population, unlike those of other types of subsample members, are associated with higher incomes and greater earnings capacity. Similarly, as we imputed the characteristics of absent fathers who were retained in the sample following a split to those who became nonrespondents, it is likely that the availability of absent fathers' resources relative to their current needs has been overestimated compared to what we might find in a truly representative group of absent fathers. Lastly, the size of our population of family splits was so small, especially when we disaggregated the subsample into classes, that generalizations based upon these findings would be highly speculative at best. Thus one should not feel free, based upon these findings, to extrapolate to the entire population of female heads and absent fathers, and certainly not to the AFDC-recipient population. The value of this exercise lies in the recognition of the magnitude of the differentials between current amounts of child support and the extent to which resources from which we might expect more support are available, no matter what measure of ability to pay is used.

Summary

We have explored the consequences, in terms of estimating the ability of the absent father to pay child support and the need for it, of two measures of economic well-being—earned income and earnings capacity. Compared with what actually happens as a consequence of the present system, our analysis suggests that there may be a considerable resource gap between absent fathers and the households containing their children by former unions. Though this gap persists into the higher income brackets, the rate of increase appears to taper off due to increasing levels of income and greater earnings capacity, and possibly higher remarriage rates, of the female heads. Thus the low child support (when measured as a percentage of income) for upper-income men which we observed earlier in this chapter, might be less inequitable than appearances would have us believe. This apparent inequity for upper-income fathers might have been reduced further had we been able to measure the value of property granted to both parties at the time of a divorce. However, as most property is granted to a female head as her share of property acquired by joint effort during the marriage, it may not properly belong in a discussion of on-going family support. Furthermore, when only the equity in a residence is granted, mortgage payments are usually the responsibility of the woman from the point of divorce onward. Even when accounting for real and personal property ownership after a split, Robert Hampton of the University of Michigan found the relative economic positions of the formerly married men and women—both with and without children—tend to become increasingly disparate over time, favoring the men.[29] When real or personal property is granted a woman in lieu of alimony the picture becomes a bit cloudier, as even the judiciary cannot agree as to the proper definition or function of alimony.[30] More to the point perhaps is that the proportion of all female heads of households who are awarded property of any consequential size at the time of marital dissolution is probably quite small, overall. Further research should certainly be directed at exploring the role of property settlements in the adjudication of child support.

What we also found in the analyses in this chapter was that there were a few absent fathers (about one to 3 percent) who can contribute nothing toward the support of their children by former unions, owing primarily to incomes which are insufficient for meeting their own needs and/or the needs of present families, but that most fathers can make some economic contribution to their former families, and this contribution might be much, much larger than has been believed possible. Nonetheless, it is unreasonable to expect child support payments to abolish the poverty of the female-headed family altogether. For those female-headed families whose pretransfer incomes place them above poverty levels, the magnitude of child support payments clearly contributes to the extent to which they are "at risk" to poverty, but their own earnings and those of subsequent husbands may have a much more substantial role in their economic independence. Whether this should be the rule is questionable, but this is a topic which will be taken up in later chapters. The fact remains that by either basic measure of economic well-being used here, there appears to be an enormous untapped source of funds that could be used to improve the economic status of children in female-headed households.

Again, however, one must keep in mind the nature of the nonrepresentativeness of the Michigan sample as discussed in chapter 2, the additional bias imparted to our subsample of family splits by the manner in which they were selected, and the probable consequences of the manipulations employed to compensate for missing data. The effects of all of this include the likely overestimate of the percentage of women who actually receive support (offset somewhat, but slightly, by the tendency of AFDC recipients to hide the fact that they receive support); overestimates of the income and earnings capacities of absent fathers, female heads, and their subsequent spouses; and underestimates of the frequency with which absent fathers remarry and/or have more children. For instance, none of the family splits had discernible illegitimate children, yet 35 percent of the entire subsample membership—45 percent of those who were female heads in the base year of the Michigan Survey and 62 percent of those who moved out of sample families at some point during the eight years of the survey—had at least one illegitimate child. We are therefore missing information on the fathers of all of the illegitimate children in our sample. If these men are able to pay less relative to the need than are fathers of legitimate children, then we have yet another source of upward bias.

In spite of the overall net effect of inflating the estimates of absent fathers' ability to pay child support and hence making our results tentative and subject to many qualifications, they are so dramatically different from the common belief that further exploration is certainly warranted. Future research should be directed at isolating a more representative population for whom complete data are available, and exploring the question of the availability of resources based upon other measures of ability to pay in addition to those developed here.

Notes

1. John L. Hauer and Clarence M. Davis, *Conservatorship,* Advanced Family Law Refresher Course, State Bar of Texas: 1976, pp. 1-5. See also John J. Sampson, "Using a Formula to Set Child Support," *Section Report, Family Law,* Vol. 77-1, State Bar of Texas: March 1977, pp. 27-28; and "Income-Percentage Scales Criticized Before Support Enforcement Officers," *The Family Law Reporter,* Vol. 3, No. 27, Text Section 11, The Bureau of National Affairs, Inc.: Washington, D.C., May 10, 1977, pp. 2423-2426.

2. Walter D. Johnson, "Divorce, Alimony, Support and Custody: A Survey of Judges' Attitudes in One State," *The Family Law Reporter:* November 9, 1976, p. 4004. See also Loy M. Simpkins, ed., *Texas Family Law,* Section 13.108, Vol. II, Speer's Fifth Edition, Bancroft-Whitney Co.: San Francisco, 1976, p. 481.

3. Sampson, "Using a Formula to Set Child Support," op. cit., pp. 27-28.

4. Doss v. Doss, 521 S.W. 2d 709-713 (Texas Civil Appeals Court Houston—14th District), 1975.

5. Harold A. Thomas, "A Practical View of Child Support and Its Collection," *Texas Bar Journal:* September 1972, pp. 791-792. See also Johnson, op. cit., pp. 4011-4012.

6. Johnson, op. cit., pp. 4011-4012.

7. Ibid., p. 12.

8. Thomas, op. cit., p. 791.

9. *The Family Law Reporter,* Vol. 3, No. 27, The Bureau of National Affairs, Inc.: Washington, D.C., May 1977, pp. 3101-3102.

10. Thomas, op. cit., p. 791.

11. John J. Sampson, "Practitioners' Estimates of Average Child Support Orders in Texas," *Section Report, Family Law,* Vol. 77-2, State Bar of Texas: June 1977, pp. 24-25.

12. Ibid.

13. Johnson, op. cit., p. 4004.

14. Thomas, op. cit., p. 792.

15. Sampson, "Using a Formula to Set Child Support," op. cit., p. 27.

16. Johnson, op. cit., p. 4003.

17. Ibid. ·

18. Betty L. Osburne, "Your Child's Keeper," *Phi Kappa Phi Journal*, Vol. 55, No. 3: Summer 1975, pp. 19-21. See also Heather L. Ross and Isabel V. Sawhill, *Time of Transition: The Growth of Families Headed by Women,* The Urban Institute: Washington, D.C., 1975, pp. 175-176; and also Alvin Schorr, "The Family Income Cycle and Income Development," *Social Security Bulletin:* February 1966, p. 24.

19. Income divided by the appropriate SSA poverty level (see Table A-13 in the Appendix) will give us a ratio for an individual or a family with which to facilitate comparisons between them. For example, a four-person family with a 1974 income of $7,000 a year would have an income-poverty ratio of 1.5 because the 1974 SSA poverty level for that type of family was $4,680. A six-person, nonfarm family with an income of $8,500 would have an income-poverty ratio of 1.2 (SSA poverty level of $7,360), indicating that in spite of a higher income the latter family was less well off than the former, relatively speaking.

20. Ross and Sawhill, op. cit., p. 113.

21. Irwin Garfinkel and Robert Haveman, "Measuring Economic Status: The Concept of Earnings Capacity," Chapter I of an unpublished manuscript, Institute for Research on Poverty, The University of Wisconsin, Madison: 1975, pp. 1-4. Used with permission of authors.

22. *The Family Law Reporter,* op. cit., p. 3102.

23. Doris L. Sassower, "No-Fault Divorce and Women's Property Rights: A Rebuttal," *New York State Bar Journal,* Vol. 45, No. 7, Nov. 1973, pp. 485-489.

24. Irwin Garfinkel and Robert Haveman, "The Measurement of Earnings Capacity," Chapter II of an unpublished manuscript, Institute for Research on Poverty, the University of Wisconsin, Madison: 1975, p. 1.

25. Irwin Garfinkel and Robert Haveman, "The Fight Against Poverty: Earnings Capacity and the Target Efficiency of Alternative Transfer Programs," reprinted from the *Journal of the American Economic Association:* May 1974, p. 197.

26. Garfinkel and Haveman, "The Measurement of Earnings Capacity," op. cit., p. 6.

27. These coefficients were calculated by Garfinkel and Haveman for other, unrelated work under way at the Institute for Research on Poverty, and were provided to the author for this analysis in 1976, for which she remains grateful.

28. Blanche Bernstein and P. Giacchino, "Costs of Daycare: Implications for Public Policy," *City Almanac:* August 1971.

29. Robert Hampton, "Marital Disruption: Some Social and Economic

Consequences," *Five Thousand American Families—Patterns of Economic Progress,* Vol. III, ed. Greg J. Duncan and James N. Morgan, Survey Research Center, The University of Michigan: 1975, p. 169.

30. Homer Clark, *The Law of Domestic Relations in the United States*; "Alimony—Historical Background," Alimony and Property Divisions, West Publishing Co., St. Paul, Minn.; 1968, Sec. 14-1: pp. 421-422.

5

State Location and Support Programs: Cost-Effectiveness in 1973, 1974, and 1975

Introduction

It will be recalled that in chapter 1 we described the development and structure of the state programs designed to identify and/or locate absent fathers for the purpose of securing support moneys from them for their dependent children. It was because of the perceived deficiencies in these state programs that federal legislation mandating reorganization and coordination of the system was deemed necessary. It will also be recalled that increasing the expenditures on location and support efforts was viewed as unavoidable in order to restructure the system, and justified on the grounds that decreases in welfare payments would exceed the extra costs entailed by expanding location and support enforcement efforts. In other words, it was anticipated that the amount of child support collections in excess of program costs would offset, dollar for dollar, AFDC expenditures. Requiring collections to exceed program costs is a good way to measure program success, if one can demonstrate which child support collections are directly attributable to program effort and if one can clearly specify all costs, both direct and indirect, of location and support enforcement. To the extent that the former condition cannot be met, benefits will be overstated. To the extent that costs, principally indirect ones, cannot be identified, the benefit-cost ratio will be inflated.

Early Studies of Cost-Effectiveness

Prior to enactment of the federal child support enforcement and parent locator service programs (Public Law 93-647) in December 1974, only one document pertaining to cost-effectiveness of state support programs was available. Case studies of the state programs of Washington and Massachusetts, selected because of demonstrated "progress in the collection of support payments," were undertaken by the Assistance Payments Administration in 1974.[1] The stated purpose was the search for alternatives for offsetting AFDC costs, which had been rising steadily in recent years due to "excessive error rates"[2] and growth of the "continued absence of a parent" category as a reason for AFDC eligibility.[3] The studies were basically descriptive and the claims for AFDC savings due to child support enforcement efforts were poorly documented. Varying periods of time were used for reporting purposes, making comparison within the states, as well as between them, impossible. The bulk of the report consisted of the reproduction of forms used by the support units. Within the document there were several empirically based conclusions, however, and among the more important were that:

1. Over a thirty-three-month period ending in March 1974, 67.8 percent of the Washington State AFDC cases were enumerated in the support unit caseload.[4] (No comparable figures were available for Massachusetts);
2. In the Massachusetts program, the average direct cost of location and support activities was six cents for every dollar collected.[5] The cost per dollar collected in Washington was twenty-two cents.[6]

A major drawback of these studies, however, was the underestimation of costs and the overestimation of collections. Costs were underestimated by a failure to measure or attempt to estimate indirect costs; for instance, perusal of forms used by support workers at the New York City Division of Location and Support indicates that information used to locate absent parents and verify employment is routinely requested from such places as the Division of Motor Vehicles, State Unemployment Division, Workman's Compensation Board, Social Security Administration, insurance companies, former employers, Department of Vital Statistics, etc.[7] These represent only a few of several sources of indirect costs. Collections had been inflated by inclusion of a miscellaneous category of collections that referred to medical, third-party, funeral, foster-care, and nonassistance recoveries. In addition, there is no way of knowing how much of the child support collections was directly attributable to support-unit activities, and how much was forthcoming prior to AFDC application and merely shifted administratively, being counted as a collection by the accounting office after an individual became an AFDC recipient. The child support recovery unit in Iowa, for instance, reported in written communications with the author that prior to setting up their state support unit in 1972, $1.2 million was contributed as child support by absent parents. They further stated that for their accounting purposes this figure represents the baseline for recoveries *without* the unit. Even this procedure is inadequate, however, unless some means is employed of accounting for a base which expands as the pool of AFDC beneficiaries expands. Or better yet, child support payments already being received by women as they enter AFDC status should not be included in collection figures unless these payments cease and public enforcement efforts must be initiated. Without this kind of a breakdown, imputed benefits in the form of collections may have been overestimated.

In 1975, Arthur Young and Company, under contract with the Social and Rehabilitation Service of the Department of Health, Education and Welfare, studied 1,317 cases of five counties' location and support programs in depth in order to help develop a model for evaluating cost-effectiveness of child support enforcement programs. These five counties—San Bernadino, Orange, and Sacramento (California), Genessee (Michigan), and the Seattle Field Office of the Washington State Office of Support Enforcement—were selected because they had been found upon preliminary investigation to be among the most successful in the country.[8] (The final report does not describe the process by which the five counties were selected. The time period under scrutiny by Young was 1964-1974, and this fact alone must have restricted the number of potential model counties as many states did not have child support units designated prior to 1969, at which time Chapter II of Title 45 of the Code of Federal Regulations mandated the organization of such units.[9])

Using two efficiency criteria, "rate of return" and "net return," the Young associates analyzed a number of aspects of the location and support process—program and agency structure, female head and absent father characteristics, legal and judicial system variables—and postulated a multiplicative model whereby program effectiveness is dependent upon success at each stage of the process. Success at each stage—intake, location, financial assessment, establishment of support, and collection and enforcement—is in turn dependent upon individual case and organizational characteristics of one sort or another. Paternity determination was dropped from the final model because the researchers claimed that those cases constituted a "negligible" portion (23 percent) of the total number (1,317) of support cases examined.[10] That 23 percent is negligible is a highly questionable assertion.

The strengths of the Young study were many. Among these were the following:

1. The necessity of measuring the indirect, as well as the direct, costs of child support enforcement programs was pointed out;[11]
2. The interdependent quality of program components was emphasized by the formulation of a multiplicative model of cost-effectiveness;[12]
3. The researchers stressed the importance of "cost-avoidance" by extending support enforcement efforts to non-welfare recipients;[13]
4. Several ways of improving overall benefit-cost ratios were mentioned, though not necessarily recommended. Among them were:
    a. "Creaming" or filtering, that is, systematically selecting cases to pursue for support that have characteristics more closely associated with greater amounts of support and high compliance rates;[14]
    b. Immediate identification and follow-up of absent fathers who miss a payment;[15] and
    c. Focus on obtaining civil court-ordered support even though it is more costly than voluntary support agreements, as the level of support ordered and compliance rates for the former offset the additional costs.[16]

As important and informative as the Young study was, there were a number of problems and limitations in evidence. The first, but not necessarily the most important, was that the researchers did not consistently employ one particular accounting period for their analytical purposes. For one analysis, the accounting period might be a year;[17] for another it might be thirty-six months.[18] As comparisons were made across periods, the reader is unsure of the value of the figures. This was further complicated by the fact that the five programs had been in operation for varying periods of time, making comparisons of performance between them at the same point in time rather tenuous. (One would think, for instance, that a program in operation for five or more years would be more cost-effective than a newer program.)

Second, confusion as to the unit of analysis prevailed throughout the study. For some purposes, the unit of analysis was the program itself or some component thereof. For other purposes it was one of the aforementioned 1,317 cases. Although it gradually becomes clear that the five counties did not work on so few cases for the entire ten-year period in question, the criteria for selecting the 1,317 cases were never mentioned. Thus, we have no way of knowing how representative they were of the total population served during the whole period. It was clearly unwarranted for the researchers to extrapolate from their findings based upon the 1,317 cases to the entire program over the ten-year period, or to make projections for programs in the future.[19] The problem was further complicated by the lack of clarification as to the source (for want of a better word) of the 1,317 cases—that is, were they the fathers of the dependent children or the mothers? Although the Young document specified in several places that there were 1,317 absent fathers, no such information is provided on the mothers. Thus we do not know how many families, if any, in this sample involve multiple fathers. We would not be concerned except for the possible bias which would have been imparted by the researchers' selection of dependent families for which there was only one absent father, or the selection of absent fathers who had only one child. We are quite suspicious that this might have been the case, as the majority (97 percent) of absent fathers were reported to have fathered only one child and the mean number of children was 1.6,[20] well below the national mean number of children per AFDC family, 2.6.[21] As most of the absent fathers in the Young sample had only one child, their ability to pay child support might be substantially greater than that of an actual cross section of fathers of AFDC-dependent children.

A third problem was that of misleading data. For instance, one particular exhibit purports to compare the costs of establishing support with the average support paid. The support paid was an average based upon the lifetime of the case, however, while the cost of securing it was a one-time-only figure which does not take into account continual or repetitive activity in the case of noncompliance.[22] One could also interpret this as a problem arising out of mixed accounting periods.

Another problem with the Young study that led to an underestimate of program costs was the failure of the researchers to heed their own advice regarding an assessment of all indirect, as well as direct, costs. While estimating these for some program components specifically, intake, location, financial assessment, collection, and enforcement, they failed to estimate the indirect costs of the program component for which indirect costs are likely the highest: the establishment of the support obligation, the part of the process which relies most heavily upon the judicial and law enforcement sectors. Similarly, the decision to exclude the paternity determination component from the benefit-cost model has the effect of underestimating (possibly to a significant extent) costs which are also largely indirect, because of the heavy reliance upon other sectors of government. In light of the expressed concern of policymakers and administrators of welfare programs with the rising incidence of illegitimacy and multiple fathers of AFDC children, the decision to exclude this component from the Young model appears unwarranted.[23]

Due to the failure of the Young researchers to include indirect costs or paternity costs in their summary table,[24] we prepared our own program cost estimates (see Table A-16 in Appendix), including the Young estimates of indirect costs when available, and determined the overall average (including paternity determination) to be $220.82 (the Young estimate was $115.42).[25] The net benefit has consequently been shrunk from $252.64 to $147.26 per case. Although this remains a positive figure, it must be restated that the Young report does *not* include any estimate of the indirect costs of the establishment of support component of the process, and we remain uncertain of the accounting periods for collection and cost measurements in general. Therefore, our own estimate of per-case cost very likely falls short of the real cost also. Just how much so remains a critical question.

It is important to the above discussion to note that the Young researchers at one point stated that 40 percent of the 1,317 cases entered active status with prior support orders.[26] If these 527 cases (a substantial number) were included when determining the average cost of the support process, and there is every indication that this is so, and if child support payments were already forthcoming from a proportion of them, then the Young estimate of average costs may be considerably deflated by the inclusion of cases for which little or no work needed to be done. This is of importance to us because we must be certain when evaluating the effectiveness of these child support enforcement programs that all collections being claimed are directly attributable to program efforts and not simply due to bookkeeping methods.

Similarly, the underlying rationale for public pursuit of child support assumes that the collections which exceed the costs—that is, the net benefits of enforcement programs—will offset, dollar for dollar, AFDC expenditures. Current federal regulations have abolished the $20-per-month maximum bonus which an AFDC recipient can keep from the child support collected on her behalf. Now, every dollar in child support which is collected for her results in a dollar reduction in her needs budget. For states which pay 100 percent of the need, this amounts to a dollar-for-dollar reduction in the AFDC grant.[27] For this reason, we must be certain that non-AFDC collections and costs are accounted for in a manner which does not make it appear that the net benefit was retained by the government to offset AFDC costs. The Young researchers presented data, however, that lead the reader to believe that non-AFDC costs and collections were not accounted for separately by the five counties over the ten-year period examined.

Furthermore, a re-analysis of some data from the Young report suggests that a disproportionate percentage of collections were comprised of non-AFDC cases (see Table A-17 in Appendix). In Genessee County, for instance, non-AFDC cases accounted for 66 percent of the child support unit caseload and 78 percent of the collections. By the Young researchers' own estimate, the net return on non-AFDC child support enforcement was demonstrably greater in all five programs than was that of AFDC cases.[28] As the counties did not really "make money" on these non-AFDC collections, the Young report should have excluded non-AFDC cases from all analyses which focused upon total program costs and benefits. Most programs charged non-AFDC recipients a small fee based upon a sliding scale to cover costs of collection. Since the new federal legislation, some states have been charging nothing for non-AFDC enforcement, and these costs have been passed on to the federal government. However, program administrators admit to not encouraging non-AFDC applications as the larger portion of the costs may eventually be borne by the states, and collections, except for small fees, will not be retained. These state officials believe that the net cost of these services to non-AFDC recipients will be substantial. As of this writing, the federal government has extended funding for child support enforcement services for this group of clients through September 30, 1978.[29]

A second alternative to the accounting problem caused by including non-AFDC collections and costs in total figures would have been to attempt to estimate the savings which are made possible by enforcing child support for these marginal cases, and thus helping to prevent their becoming active AFDC recipients. Although the Young researchers did not do this, we believe it is critical to be able to measure this savings effect in order to evaluate these programs in the future.

Finally, the Young report neglected to present an estimate of the marginal rate of return which we might expect on expenditures for location and support efforts. If the amount of collections is a direct consequence of the amount of expenditure, as the Young researchers assert[30] and as policymakers apparently believe, then we would need to know how much more we might expect in collections for every additional dollar put into child support enforcement programs. A serious oversight on the part of the Young researchers was that they failed to give the reader data with which to compare the rate of growth in collections and the rate of growth in program costs over the ten-year period. They did, however, offer the following: over fiscal years 1964-1974, average annual rates of growth in AFDC-related collections ranged from 13.9 percent to 26.9 percent,[31] and average annual rates of increase in staff levels, in which more than half of the personnel were professionals, ranged from 11.6 percent to 20.6 percent.[32] Increased staffs and increasing proportions of professionals probably meant rapid increases in direct costs, 81 percent of which were attributable to salaries.[33] We cannot say for certain, due to the data limitations previously described, but it does not seem improbable that rates of growth in costs exceeded those of collections.

It is quite likely that more extensive analysis of public child support enforcement programs would reveal a declining rate of return on the investment in such activities. It would be of great help to be able to predict at what point one might expect further effort (expenditure) to be of no net value, reflecting the proportion of absent fathers who are too poor, transient, and determined not to pay to ever be worth the cost of enforcement. Also, the Young data itself suggests that given a nonreplacing sample (the same persons over time), collections appear to fall off faster than do the costs of enforcement monitoring.[34] That is, after initially high costs, which then fall off but must remain constant in order to insure continued compliance, the marginal rate of return per case diminishes because arrearages which are seldom fully recovered accumulate, and unlike program costs child support payments are not usually readjusted or readjudicated to keep abreast of inflation.

In summary, then, we have been led by an analysis of the Young report to an identification of several problem areas in terms of measuring the cost-effectiveness of publically financed child support enforcement programs. Among these are:

1. The choice of appropriate and internally consistent accounting periods and units of analysis;
2. The identification and measurement of all indirect costs of these programs, especially those which incur public costs;
3. The distinction between collections which are due to program effort and those which would have been forthcoming for reasons independent of public enforcement efforts;
4. The estimation of AFDC savings due to enforcement of child support for marginal cases; and finally,
5. The importance of "creaming" or filtering and its relationship to marginal rates of return on the public investment in these programs.

The Marginal Rate of Return on Six State Child Support Program Expenditures—Fiscal Years 1973-1975

Clearly, from the preceding discussion, there still remain a number of unanswered questions pertaining to the expected return on a public investment in child support enforcement.

In an attempt to address the last of those issues posed above, that of the marginal rate of return on program expenditures, we set out to obtain from as many states as possible cost and collection figures for the three years prior to implementation of the new federal program. From a staff publication of the U.S. Senate Finance Committee, we were able to identify states for which cost and collection figures were presented for all three years in question.[35] When contacted, many of these states' program administrators were either unaware of how the figures were obtained by the Finance Committee staff or were unable to reproduce them. However, we were able to get cost and collection figures from six states—Georgia, Iowa, Maine, Massachusetts, Oregon, and Tennessee—for fiscal years 1973, 1974, and 1975, from which much of Table 5-1 was generated. It is clear from this table that the state programs appear to be quite cost-effective, with benefit-cost ratios averaging 8.54, 8.02, and 8.03 for the three years respectively. It should be noted that these ratios are average, though, and we still need estimates of the marginal rates of return, to which we now turn our attention.

The Predictive Model

In order to maximize the number of observations, yet minimize the problem of intercorrelation of the error terms that would be the consequence of violating the assumption of independence across years within states, we employed a first- and second-differences method to analyze our state data. Thus we subtracted 1973 collections from 1974 collections, and 1974 collections from 1975 collections (and so forth, for child support enforcement program costs and AFDC costs), for a total of twelve observation points (see Table 5-2).[36]

Our predictive model states simply that child support collections by the states are a linear function of the dollars invested in the support programs, controlling for AFDC expenditures in those states. See Tables A-18 in the Appendix for the regression formula. Our model includes the control variable AFDC expenditures so that we can estimate the impact of child support enforcement programs independent of AFDC costs. The reason for including AFDC expenditures in our model is that larger states would likely have both greater AFDC costs and higher child support enforcement costs and collections, all other things being equal.

Results

Child support collections regressed on child support enforcement program costs and AFDC expenditures produced the following results, summarized in Table 5-3.

Table 5-1
Costs and Collections: Child Support Enforcement Programs in Six States, 1973, 1974, and 1975

State	F.Y. 1973			F.Y. 1974			F.Y. 1975		
	Costs (Direct Only)	Collections	Total AFDC[a] Payments Computable for Federal Funding	Costs (Direct Only)	Collections	Total AFDC Payments Computable for Federal Funding	Costs (Direct Only)	Collections	Total AFDC Payments Computable for Federal Funding
Georgia	69,978.00	38,282.00	119,543,779	223,583.00	1,823,951.00	128,654,628	303,000	3,227,671.00	134,476,843
Iowa	99,042.00	1,156,465.91	52,999,211	296,563.00	1,718,070.00	55,756,623	400,000	2,953,735.00	79,485,821
Maine	154,880.49	703,901.10	32,821,442	188,346.00	790,476.95	35,601,678	199,545	908,941.77	47,379,653
Massachusetts	739,384.61	17,015,723.00	287,283,337	1,000,090.00	18,600,000.00	330,561,646	1,316,800	21,300,000.00	394,094,286
Oregon	771,832.00	2,957,155.00	47,165,418	862,782.00	3,424,417.00	63,063,313	1,036,000	4,637,799.00	76,393,947
Tennessee	69,488.06	529,812.27	70,311,658	73,057.83	541,772.58	71,433,576	78,911.09	546,500.22	78,246,682

Note: Caution is in order for interpreting table 5-1. The child support collection figures for at least Tennessee, and likely the others as well, include payments made by absent parents to the state as partial reimbursement for foster-care services. To some extent the inclusion of this kind of payment distorts the picture if our policy focus is upon reduction of AFDC costs through enforcement of the absent father's support obligation. Similarly, it is likely that collections (and possibly costs as well) include those for non-AFDC cases, the consequences of which have already been discussed. In addition, it is important to add that the program costs specified in Table 5-1 are in every case direct costs only.

aSource: *Fiscal Year* [1973, 1974, 1975]: *State Expenditures for Public Assistance Programs Approved Under Titles I, IV-A, X, XIV, XVI, and XIX of the Social Security Act;* Department of Health, Education, and Welfare, Social and Rehabilitation Service, Information Systems, Washington, D.C.

Table 5-2
First and Second Differences

State	Year	Collections	Child Support Program Costs	AFDC Expenditures
Georgia				
	1974-1973	$1,785,669	$153,605	$ 9,110,859
	1975-1974	1,293,720	79,417	5,822,215
Iowa				
	1974-1973	561,605	197,521	2,757,412
	1975-1974	1,235,665	103,437	23,729,198
Maine				
	1974-1973	86,575	33,466	2,780,236
	1975-1974	118,465	11,199	11,777,975
Massachusetts				
	1974-1973	1,584,277	260,706	43,278,309
	1975-1974	2,700,000	316,710	63,533,640
Oregon				
	1974-1973	467,262	90,950	15,897,895
	1975-1974	1,213,382	173,218	13,330,634
Tennessee				
	1974-1973	11,960	3,569	1,121,918
	1975-1974	4,728	5,854	6,813,106

Both costs of enforcement and AFDC expenditures appear to have an impact upon child support collections. Controlling for the effect of the size of AFDC expenditures, these programs returned almost seven dollars in child support for every dollar spent on enforcement. This is almost as great as the *average* rates of return. Even with the possibility of distortions in the data produced by an overestimation of collections and an underestimation of costs, it is likely that the marginal rate of return on child support enforcement programs for those six states was still quite good.

Though not producing a statistically significant coefficient, there also appeared to have been some effect on collections produced by the size of the AFDC expenditure. The AFDC F-ratio, 1.369, suggests an impact in the predicted direction upon child support collections, though admittedly not a statistically significant one. Coupled with the fact that the value of the standard error of regression coefficient was so close to that of the beta itself, it is hard to ignore the possibility that some relationship exists between child support collections and AFDC expenditures which is independent of the effect of enforcement costs. Such an effect may be the consequence of providing an expanded pool of AFDC recipients from which to filter cases that appear to have characteristics associated with higher support payments.

Table 5-3
Child Support Collections

Independent Variables	Regression Coefficient	Standard Error of Regression Coefficient	F-Value	Significance Level
Child Support Enforcement Costs	6.717	2.032	6.717	.029
AFDC Expenditures	.013	.011	1.369	.272

In addition to this model, we ran three other regression equations, the results of which generally confirmed our original finding of cost-effectiveness. In the first instance, regressing child support collections on program costs but using each year for every state (eighteen observations) as observation points, the coefficient for our independent variable was 13.30, indicating a return of $13 for each dollar invested in location and support enforcement (see Table A-18 in the Appendix). When using the first- and second-differences method again, but adding a set of dummy variables to control for the state effect, the coefficient for program costs dropped to 4.864, the F-value for which was only of marginal magnitude (see Table A-19 in the Appendix). Lastly, and again using the first- and second-differences method, we regressed collections on costs, AFDC expenditures, and the state dummies. In this instance, the coefficients for AFDC expenditures and support enforcement costs were both highly significant (see Table A-20 in the Appendix), and the latter indicated that over five dollars could be expected for each dollar spent on enforcement programs, controlling for the other factors.

Recent Evidence from the New Federal Program

As of this writing, cost and collections data from the new federalized location and support program are incomplete. While some states' programs have been in existence since July 1, 1975, many were still not completely operant by July 1977.[37] Thus program costs during these early, "start-up" months may be much higher than they will be after the program has been in operation for a few years. During the first fiscal year of the federal program, 987,879 AFDC and 625,202 non-AFDC cases were processed for an average of $240.98 in support collected.[38] During the first two quarters of fiscal year 1977, however, 645,785

AFDC and 623,541 non-AFDC cases were processed for a per-case collection of $24.84! Either the government figures are faulty or else the point of diminishing returns has already been reached. The more recent set of figures indicates further that $27.37 was collected per non-AFDC case. The ratio of collections to costs was 2.61 for the AFDC group, but only 1.19 for the non-AFDC group.[39] These costs are those borne by the states and the federal government for the operation of the program at the state level; we have no information as to the cost of the Federal Office of Child Support Enforcement and the Parent Locator Service.

Many of the problems cited earlier in respect to the data gathered by the Arthur Young researchers and the prefederal state data which this author analyzed remain regarding the most recent, federal figures. Specifically,

1. We still have no clear notion of collections over the life of an enforcement case;
2. We do not know what proportion of the child support collections for AFDC recipients were a direct consequence of public enforcement activity;
3. We do not know what portion of non-AFDC collections represents savings as a consequence of preventing AFDC dependence; and possibly most critically,
4. We still do not know the extent to which the reported administrative costs of these programs reflect the real costs, both direct and indirect.

Admittedly, the answers to most of the above questions will be extraordinarily difficult to derive. In fact, the answers may not be worth the effort of obtaining them. It may be that we know all that is important to know about these programs already. That is, after all costs are accounted for and no collections are counted that are not directly attributable to program effort, the child support enforcement program may turn out to be of marginal economic value. The more important question, then, might well turn out to be, Why, if absent parents are able to contribute more than they presently are contributing, are we not able to tap that resource more fully?

Conclusion

Even after all possible adjustments have been made with admittedly limited data, we are left with a great many doubts as to the potential cost-effectiveness of the present child support enforcement programs. On the one hand, our experience with the state programs which preceded the federal program suggests that this effort can be cost-effective, perhaps as a direct result of "creaming"—a practice that is no longer allowed as a consequence of the federal legislation. On the other hand, evidence from the new federal program, which is now two years old, suggests that the public child support enforcement effort may be of only marginal value, if any at all, if program administrators concern themselves merely with the net return. "Creaming" is clearly inequitable as it implies that the full force of the law will be brought to bear upon only those who possess demographic characteristics associated with better payment performance. If, however, maximal child support enforcement activities are applied to all absent parents, regardless of demographic characteristics, the concept of cost-effectiveness which is the consequence of a reduction in AFDC expenditures loses meaning—first because there will always be some absent parents for whom the costs of the pursuit of child support through the cumbersome, time-consuming legal-judicial system will never be outweighed by the collections, and second because the savings which result from averting AFDC dependency can never be accurately measured, no matter how sophisticated the methods of cost/benefit estimation or projection.

It is possible, however, to avoid this dilemma by adopting a policy stance that is not based upon a cost-effectiveness rationale, but rather views the public enforcement of the child support obligation as a fundamental function of society.

Notes

1. "How They Do It," *Child Support Payments Control, Massachusetts and Washington,* Assistance Payments Administration, Social and Rehabilitation Service, Department of Health, Education and Welfare: Washington, D.C., 1974, p. 1.

2. Ibid., Preface.

3. Ibid., p. 1.

4. Ibid., p. 71.

5. Ibid., p. 10.

6. Ibid., p. 52.

7. *Handbook for Caseworkers in Division of Location and Support,* New York City Human Resources Administration, Department of Social Services: April 1975, pp. 21-25.

8. *Detailed Summary of Findings: Absent Parent Child Support Cost-Benefit Analysis,* Arthur Young and Company, prepared under Contract No. SRS-74 56, Social and Rehabilitation Service, Department of Health, Education and Welfare: December 1975, p. 1.

9. "How They Do It," op. cit., p. 4.

10. *Detailed Summary of Findings,* op. cit., p. 54.

11. Ibid., p. 24.

12. Ibid., p. 73.

13. Ibid., p. 78.

14. The researchers, though admitting that filtering contributes to im-

proved benefit-cost ratios, advised against the practice on grounds that too much in potential collections was foregone. This would be consistent with the Arthur Young and Company accounting bias that favored maximizing net return rather than rate of return as the measure of cost-effectiveness. See *Detailed Summary of Findings,* op. cit., p. 65.

15. Ibid., p. 63.

16. Ibid., Exhibit 48.

17. Ibid., Exhibit 44.

18. Ibid., p. 68 and pp. 78-80.

19. Ibid., p. 71.

20. Ibid., Exhibit 17.

21. Lottie Lee Crafton, *Aid to Families with Dependent Children: National and Texas,* prepared for Texas Department of Public Welfare at the Center for Social Work, University of Texas at Austin: 1976, p. 82.

22. *Detailed Summary of Findings,* op. cit., p. 62.

23. The percentage of cases in which paternity was an issue ranged from 37.9 in Genessee County, Michigan, to 10.1 in the Seattle Field Office, for an average of 23.4 percent—by no means inconsequential. See *Detailed Summary of Findings,* op. cit., p. 54.

24. Ibid., p. 77.

25. Ibid., p. 71.

26. Ibid., p. 59.

27. *Policies and Procedures Manual,* Texas State Department of Public Welfare, Child Support Handbook: November 1975.

28. *Detailed Summary of Findings,* op. cit., p. 27.

29. *An Act, H.R. 1404,* Report No. 95-298, Calendar No. 276, Ninety-fifth Congress, First Session: p. 2. See also *A Bill, H.R. 7200,* Report No. 95-394, Calendar No. 220, Ninety-fifth Congress, First Session: p. 48.

30. *Detailed Summary of Findings,* op. cit., p. 79.

31. Ibid., p. 16.

32. Ibid., p. 18.

33. Ibid., p. 24.

34. Ibid., pp. 71-72.

35. *Child Support Data and Materials,* Appendix IX, prepared by the staff for the Committee on Finance, United States Senate, U.S. Government Printing Office: Washington, D.C., November 10, 1975, p. 151.

36. Special thanks to Robert M. Hauser of the Department of Sociology, University of Wisconsin, Madison, for suggesting that this method be employed to maximize usefulness of the data.

37. *First Annual Report to the Congress on the Child Support Enforcement Program,* Office of Child Support Enforcement, Department of Health, Education and Welfare: June 30, 1976. Also First and Second Quarter Fiscal Year 1977 data, Office of Child Support Enforcement, Department of Health, Education and Welfare.

38. Ibid., pp. 121, 129, and 133.

39. First and Second Quarter Fiscal Year 1977 data, op. cit.

**Part II
The Normative Issues:
How Should the Child
Support Enforcement
System be Reformed?**

6

The Child Support Enforcement System: Evidence in Support of Reform

Introduction

It has been our overall purpose in the preceding pages to pose and answer some basic questions surrounding the issue of child support enforcement policy. From chapters 1 through 5, we have concluded that:

1. Female-headed families containing children less than eighteen years of age are increasingly more likely to be poor than any other type of family and as a consequence often require income supplementation from sources outside the immediate family unit.

2. Empirical evidence suggests that whether or not child support is contributed by an absent father, and if so in what amounts, does not appear to be related to the extent of need on the part of the family unit containing the dependent children. Similarly, the relationship between the availability of resources and the amount of child support paid by the absent father turns out not to be as strong as had been predicted. The amount of variance left unexplained by a socioeconomic model suggests that the child support enforcement system is dominated by a great deal of discretion, though the precise locuses of that discretion are presently unknown.

3. The average amount of child support payments in 1974 for our national sample of female heads of families containing children less than eighteen years of age was far less than half of the poverty level that year for those families, even though 93 percent of the absent fathers had incomes that were twice (or greater than twice) the poverty level for their current families.

4. Of the 30 percent of absent fathers who paid any support at all in 1974, the percentage of absent father's income which was paid for the support of minor children in the care of their mothers appeared to be regressive, with poor and near-poor men paying child support which represented larger percentages of their earnings than did that of higher-income men.

5. It was demonstrated that an average of $3,566 might be assumed to be available to each dependent family under a formula designed to reduce the disparity in relative economic well-being between absent fathers and their former families, when income alone was used as a measure of economic well-being of both family units. When estimates of earnings capacity were used as the measure of economic well-being, the available resources drop to $2,933, which is still substantially higher than the average child support which we found to result from the present system—$539. It is necessary once again to remind the reader

that for the reasons specified in chapter 4, these figures are not likely to hold for the population in general, as our subsample population possessed atypically high socioeconomic characteristics. Thus these estimates are likely biased upwards to a significant extent, though not enough to render meaningless our overall finding of extensive untapped resources that greatly exceed the amount of child support which is being contributed under the present system.

6. If all indirect costs of child support enforcement programs were to be accounted for, and no collections that were not attributable to public effort were to be counted, there remain doubts that present child support enforcement programs can be cost-effective under a system which relies upon the pool of AFDC recipients for its clientele, especially if "creaming" or filtering of cases according to socioeconomic characteristics is not employed.

In sum, then, the evidence thus far casts serious doubt upon the efficacy of the total system of enforcing the child support obligation, in terms of both effectiveness and equity. The assertion that much of the unexplained variance in our predictive models (see chapter 3) is the consequence of a great deal of discretion at some critical juncture in the child support system, or, as is more likely, at *several* junctures in the system, is based upon a number of factors. First, although we earlier assumed that female heads would rather have child support than not, there are bound to be those who have personal reasons for preferring to support their children by themselves, with help from other relatives and/or welfare when necessary. Among these might be:

1. AFDC and Medicaid recipients, some of whom currently face a 100 percent implicit tax rate on child support in many states;[1]
2. Those who fear harassment or even physical abuse from the absent parent as a consequence of taking legal action for support;
3. Some women who may be uncertain as to the identity of the father of a child; and
4. Those women who might find it too embarrassing or costly, in both real and personal terms, to pursue child support through the legal system.

Among low-income, female-headed families, these reasons for preferring not to pursue support might prevail among the majority. The Young study, it will be recalled, found that only 40 percent of its sample of enforcement cases entered active status with prior orders for support,[2] which indicates that among a low-income population for whom costs of litigation are relatively more burdensome, there may exist considerably less demand for child support than among the nonpoor population of female heads of families. The Young finding does not necessarily contradict our own findings, reported in chapter 3, that the earnings of a female head are not a significant independent predictor of child support receipt. Following family dissolution, it is likely that a low-income female head will first apply for welfare before engaging an attorney and beginning the legal effort to secure child support, especially if she knows that the welfare department will provide her with that service. Given this, the Young finding that 40 percent of those welfare recipients who were referred for child support enforcement services had prior court orders for support could be viewed as a rather large percentage.

Although there may be other reasons why some women might prefer to bear the entire cost of child-rearing, or share that cost with the public, the above probably represent the chief reasons why some custodial parents might not want to receive any support from the absent parent. Though we presently do not know the extent to which these four reasons for not pursuing support are found in the population of child support eligibles, intelligent planning requires that we consider all possible responses to the child support enforcement opportunity. Future research should be directed at continuing inquiry into all aspects of the problem, including but not limited to the role of the above four factors in determining the extent to which custodial parents take advantage of the child support enforcement system.

Unwillingness of the absent parent to pay support, together with the cumbersome, costly, and ineffective nature of the judicial system, is the more probable explanation for our findings of infrequent incidence and low levels of child support payments than are the above possibilities. If absent parents were paying as much as they could and courts and enforcement systems were more responsive, it is unlikely that we would have found such large discrepancies between what is actually being paid and what is potentially available. Other research has found that the relative well-being of absent fathers remains essentially unaffected by marital dissolution, while even after child support and alimony payments are included in the measure the relative well-being of the female-headed family is apt to be considerably lower than that of the former spouse, and this discrepancy persists over time, often ending only with the remarriage of the female head.[3] Given our own findings of such large differences in well-being between absent fathers and female heads (the largest amount of child support and alimony in our subsample was $6,000 per year), paid by a father whose income exceeded $36,000 per year and the magnitude of surplus income which is available at all income levels, we must dismiss most tales told by absent fathers that they are being economically crippled by the burden of child support payments.

Much of the unexplained variance in our predictive models can probably be attributed to the child support enforcement and judicial systems, also. Why, one might ask, should we find 40 percent of a sample of eligible families in need of public support enforcement services when they already have standing court orders for support?[4] ("Eligible" as used here means that a child has been born to a woman, which in turn means that there exists somewhere a natural father. Similarly, it is assumed that most adopted children have adoptive fathers who are legally responsible for providing support, even after marital dissolution.) How and where did the private system fail? One possible answer lies in the costs. For instance, minimal charges for attorney fees, filing costs, and so forth currently add up to $145 on a fee-for-service basis for non-AFDC recipients using the public child support enforcement service in Texas.[5] It is unlikely that the private sector can provide this service any more cheaply, or that very many attorneys in the marketplace would take on a case for so little remuneration, even if most female heads of families had such limited resources to employ in this endeavor. Even in the event a court order for support is obtained, compliance with the order is often the exception rather than the rule. As a series of articles in the Chicago *Daily News* in 1973 pointed out, the fact that only 38 percent of fathers were in full compliance with court-ordered support in Cook County[6] was attributable to the reluctance of attorneys to represent women trying to collect support, the price of such legal action (which usually must be paid in advance), and the enormous backlog of cases due to crowded dockets, which causes months of delay. Given the requirement that three months of nonpayment must have elapsed before legal action can be initiated against an absent father, a woman and her children might go for months without child support before a hearing can be held.[7] This situation is not peculiar to Cook County, Illinois, but prevails throughout the country.

A recent analysis of one hundred child support files in Travis County, Texas, found that almost half (49 percent) of the absent fathers had paid less than 10 percent of their court-ordered child support and that 19 percent had never paid any of the ordered support. This appalling situation persists in spite of the provision of free enforcement services and frequent court action against the noncompliant parent.[8] These findings are not necessarily inconsistent with our own (reported in chapter 3), which found the passage of time since the split to have no significant impact upon the level of support received, all other things being equal, in 1975. Most of the absent parents in the Travis County study apparently established their payment patterns soon after the original court order (if not before), and followed that pattern over the ten-year period being examined regardless of any court action for noncompliance that might have ensued. A smaller proportion (about 25 percent) of absent parents showed improvement in payment performance following court action for noncompliance, suggesting that there exists a small but not insignificant proportion of absent fathers who are responsive to legal coercion.[9] On the other hand, by far the greatest proportion (75 percent) appear to be beyond the ability of the enforcement system to secure support. For the most part, the evidence suggests that the legal-judicial enforcement system is ineffective in its well-intentioned, but limited, ability to enforce the parental child support obligation.[10]

Much of the failure on the part of the courts is attributable to their inability to initiate action against a noncompliant parent. Because the courts and public enforcement agencies are seldom vested with such authority, a "sieve effect" has developed, which permits absent parents who are highly mobile (or doggedly determined to avoid paying any more support than they are forced to pay) to escape. The requirement that custodial parents initiate action for noncompliance, the procedural boondoggle,[11] and delays due to excessive demand for court time contribute to the strategy whereby the absent parent minimizes the total amount of support he pays by reinstating payments just short of a court appearance. Seldom, however, are arrearages fully paid.

The relatively limited power that courts have for enforcing their support orders contributes to the problem. A family-court judge has little leverage with which to encourage compliance. Garnishment of wages, fine, and/or incarceration are the most powerful devices to which the courts can resort, but state law varies considerably on the extent to which these can be used to collect alimony and child support. The Texas state constitution prohibits garnishment for *any* purpose. Connecticut, on the other hand, exempts only $25 per week in earnings from garnishment for the purpose of support, and Indiana will not exempt any portion of a person's income when a court order exists to the contrary.[12]

Even in states with few limitations on their use, the willingness of individual judges to use these devices to enforce the child support obligation varies a great deal. Long delays between cessation of support and garnishment, when it is allowed under state law, result in accumulated arrearages which may never be caught up. Incarceration for nonsupport is seldom used by the courts for rather obvious reasons—as no support can be expected to be forthcoming while a man is in jail (during which time he may lose his job), judges are naturally reluctant to impose jail sentences for the purpose of enforcing support. For the mother of the dependent children the real and emotional costs of pursuing arrearages from a recalcitrant father are certainly formidable, and given long delays in judicial process due to overburdened civil courts,[13] it is quite probable that at this juncture the system is most ineffectual in delivering the maximum, most reasonable and equitable amount of child support to the dependent family.

Further evidence in support of reform measures directed at the mechanism for enforcing the support obligation includes our finding that support for minority children is significantly lower than support for white children. (Of 385 minority families, only forty-seven received any support during 1974. Child support averaged $958 per family for those forty-seven, or $117 per family among all 385 families. Comparable figures for whites are that seventy-seven out of 198 families received support averaging $3,360, or $1,307 for all 198 families!) Furthermore, whether or not any support at all was received was found to be partially a function of the minority or majority status of the child, with 39 percent of white families receiving support and only 12 percent of minority families receiving any support. That child support payments for minority children should be so much lower than those for white children is an inequity of serious concern, reflecting very poorly upon the present enforcement system.

Some of the above problems, many of which have been identified by analysis or review of data which are two or more years old, would be moot were it not for the fact that the most recent evidence from the Office of Child Support Enforcement suggests that problems still abound under the new federal program. Legislative obstacles at the local level, such as statutes of limitations on parternity suits,[14] prohibitions against wage assignments,[15] and lengthy judicial backlogs and lack of judicial cooperation,[16] plague the administrators of state programs. Privately, administrators of these programs have admitted that six-month lags between requests for information and responses from other states via the federal Parent Locator Service are routine. By the time the information is received, it is often too old to be useful. In addition, the average amount of money which we determined in chapter 4 was available from the fathers of AFDC children was $3,494—much, much larger than the mean figures of $240.98 collected by the state programs in the first three quarters of fiscal year 1976, and $27 in the first half of fiscal year 1977 (these are the *gross* means, not the net, and in no way reflect the costs of the programs[17])—suggesting that even with federalization, a great deal more potential money is available from absent fathers than is presently being tapped.

Furthermore, the states are required to demonstrate that child support collections exceed program costs, yet federal accounting regulations state that they may not include collections for former AFDC recipients in their cost-effectiveness figures beyond six months following grant termination, as these no longer represent any AFDC savings. Program administrators confess that this builds in an incentive to pursue only $69 in child support if $70 renders a person ineligible for AFDC. In the event the recipient is a beneficiary of other transfers which are contingent upon her AFDC status, the recipient, the program administrators, and the absent father have the same interest—to keep child support payments lower than they might otherwise be.

In addition, we have no evidence that payment performance by absent fathers whose children reside in nonpoor households is significantly improved from what it was in 1974 before the federalization of child support enforcement. Even though the states are required to provide location and support services for non-AFDC recipients on a fee-for-service basis, the best that federal and state accounts can show is that they break even on these types of cases, as they are not supposed to make a profit. That is, non-AFDC collections in excess of costs are not to be used to offset the AFDC costs, but are to be passed on directly to the non-AFDC program participants. Because of the federal requirement that the states demonstrate cost-effectiveness of their programs, serving such clients does not improve overall cost-effectiveness figures at all. Some state program administrators admitted in private conversation that non-AFDC recipients were largely ignored, though this was often difficult as these women, who stood to benefit the most from enforcement, were quite persistent in their efforts to get help. What is likely, then, is that near-poor women are probably excluded from the child support enforcement system to a greater extent than are poor women, for whom the public provides enforcement services, and others, whose incomes are high enough for them to secure costly legal services in the private sector.

Finally, because AFDC applicants and recipients are required to cooperate with child support enforcement program administrators in identifying and locating the fathers of their children, several possible violations of civil liberties are entailed. Privacy is not only invaded during the routine interview process when questions of paternity are involved, but administrators of at least one state program require lie-detector tests of some AFDC mothers when the alleged father denies paternity. The rationale for this demeaning practice is economic—it might save the state the cost of expensive blood and genetic testing to rule out the possibility of paternity. (Paternity cannot be established, or proven, by these tests, which can only establish that an individual is *not* the father of a particular child.) It is clear that another, possibly more important, purpose is served by this practice: to discourage some women from applying for or continuing to receive AFDC benefits. The practice also may serve to protect the child support enforcement programs from invasion-of-privacy suits from men who may or may not turn out to be the natural fathers of these children; it is easier for program administrators to require lie-detector tests and other evidence from the AFDC applicants and recipients because they need the AFDC and Medicaid benefits for economic survival and thus are less apt than the alledged fathers to protest this kind of treatment. Those who do not "truly need" AFDC will be kept off the rolls. Whether this method of rationing benefits is justified on any grounds, even economic ones, is questionable.

For women who fear physical reprisal from the fathers of their children, the cooperation requirements are clearly untenable. But even for women who have less socially acceptable reasons for protecting the identity and/or location of the fathers of their children, we must seriously question the legitimacy of the means by which child support enforcement program administrators get this information.

In general, then, the evidence suggests that across income classes child support payments are low (both in relation to considerations of the absent father's ability to pay and the needs of the dependent family) and unreliable. Furthermore, this appears to be due to a multiplicity of obstacles to the adjudication process, highly variable amounts of child support actually being paid, and lack of an automatic and efficient mechanism for keeping the support coming once it begins. In addition, inequities abound, to the end that persons with different demographic and personal characteristics are subject to different constraints and opportunities vis-à-vis the child support enforcement system.

Prior to discussing how some of these problems might be addressed, we turn to an exposition of values that have a direct effect upon our perception of the issues and the chosen course of action for their resolution.

Rights and Responsibilities

Two fundamental rights of the child in a home from which one parent (either natural or adoptive) is absent, are represented here: the right to be supported by both parents to the extent they are able to contribute to that support, and the right to an appropriate ranking in the priority structure of those parents. These rights apply also, the author believes, to children who live with nonrelatives and relatives who are not their parents, but for the purposes of this text attention is focused upon those children who live with one parent, as they represent by far the majority of children who do not live in intact families. It is our belief in the preeminence under most circumstances of these two rights, above those of parents to protect their privacy and choose how to spend their earnings, which underlies much of the discussion which follows.

Because an adequate family income is such an important determinant of a child's mental and physical health, intellectual functioning, and adult success, and these in turn have serious implications for society as a whole, we feel strongly that it is an appropriate public function to pursue programs and policies which will enhance family income and the reliability of that income. For a number of reasons, however, we feel that major emphasis should be given to facilitating intrafamily transfers—child support payments made by absent parents (usually fathers) to help support their minor children.

Among these reasons is the rising cost of the social dependence that is the direct consequence of family dissolution. By itself this fact does not mandate reform or restructuring of the child support system, nor should it be the basic rationale underlying public child support enforcement policy. However, given our findings of such large income surpluses in the control of absent fathers (chapter 4), some portion of the public cost of that dependence could probably be reduced by an efficient child support enforcement effort. This effort need not be viewed as a substitute for the public commitment to maintain a minimum standard of living for dependent children, although much of the past and present rationale for increasing the scope of and investment in public child support enforcement has been based upon the assumption that every dollar collected in support in excess of the costs of collection will offset a dollar of welfare expenditures. Thus, those who are committed to fostering a sense of public responsibility for economically deprived children may see in the enforcement of parental responsibility the denial of public responsibility.

This need not be the case. An emphasis upon enforcement of the parental support obligation does not necessarily result in a diminution of public concern for the welfare of children. In fact, public policy that fosters fulfillment of the obligation to support one's own children may promote a sense of responsibility which spills over into policies and practices that affect the lives of children who are not one's own. On the other hand, policies that perpetuate the singular rationale for support enforcement to reduce AFDC costs tend to work against the promotion of public commitment to securing the economic welfare of children. Such policies include the focus of child support enforcement efforts on AFDC recipients, to the virtual neglect of nonrecipients. Also, the insistence that child support be implicitly taxed at a 100 percent rate vis-à-vis the AFDC grant, for the purpose of demonstrating cost-effectiveness, contributes to both questionable enforcement practices and a reduction in the public commitment to the welfare of children.

Furthermore, a dual support enforcement system—one which treats the children of the poor quite differently from those of the nonpoor—is prima facie inequitable. That the public should enforce economic responsibility for only one group of absent parents violates the principle of horizontal equity, in that it effectively promotes the right of poor children to be supported by their absent parents while doing little or nothing to protect that same right for nonpoor children, relying mainly upon the private sector to safeguard their rights. This inequitable situation might not exist, nor would the necessity for public intervention across income classes, were the private system for child support enforcement functioning optimally for the nonpoor. On the contrary, our results from chapter 4 analyses indicate that at all income levels child support payments are intolerably low (and too often nonexistent) when compared with the income and needs of both parents. It is well within the purview of government to insure equal treatment under the law in regard to the child support obligation, regardless of income class.

Our final set of values, by no means purely distinct from those stated above, asserts that the enforcement of familial responsibility is a proper and desirable function of government. That one half of the parental population (the noncustodial parent) should be allowed to effectively avoid such a large proportion of responsibility for its offspring by shifting that responsibility to other relatives and nonrelatives is untenable in a society that has the technological capability for preventing much of the shift.

Bearing in mind the value position stated above, a tentative proposal for child support reform is being offered for consideration. In so doing, we have decided that certain rights and principles must be given priority over others. Part of the decisions involving the ordering of priorities stem from our personal values, and part from a rational assessment of the real and social costs of continuing the present system—the public-private mix—of child support enforcement.

It is our view that the adequacy of child support payments, the equity, and the enforcement of responsibility of child support policy should be given primacy in the evaluation of the existing system and proposals for reform. In an unpublished working paper in 1976, Harold Watts stipulated that the principles of adequacy, equity, and responsibility be emphasized in reforming enforcement policies in conjunction with an overhaul of the income maintenance system.[18] These should outweigh concerns such as the right to privacy, freedom of choice as to which children (if any) an absent father should support and to what extent, and the sanctity of judicial discretion in determining levels of child support. In keeping with the objective of maximizing these three principles, it is necessary to consider basic and far-reaching reform of the entire child support enforcement system, as the present system is neither adequate or equitable, nor does it consistently foster parental responsibility.

The following specific changes are proposed:

1. That child support enforcement policy be directed at fostering an equal sharing of the personal and economic responsibility by both parents of a child (discussion of the specifics of this part of the proposed system forms the core of chapter 7);
2. That child support payments be made mandatory across all income classes;
3. That the full force of federal law and the appropriate machinery of government be engaged to insure that this transfer is effected in a manner which is not capricious, discriminatory, or highly discretionary; and finally,
4. That the payment of support be facilitated by an automatic process through the payroll office of the absent parent's employer, in a fashion similar to the withholding of other federal taxes.

Implementation

Several factors must be given consideration when evaluating the economic and political issues surrounding implementation of these proposed changes. Among these are the interface with the present and proposed income-maintenance/tax structure, the anticipated public costs of such a program, the consequences for the legal-judicial system, and the probable public reaction.

First, the interface with the income-maintenance/tax system would be quite logical and much easier if we were to adopt some form of guaranteed income for all families, including those with male heads, as opposed to the multiplicity of cash and in-kind transfer programs which we now provide. With changes in the income-maintenance/tax system such as those recently proposed by the Carter Administration, child support transfers could become an integrated part of the system. The custodial parent might have the option that the child support transfer be applied to his or her income-tax liability, deposited in a bank account (as are some Social Security benefits), sent directly to him or her on some optional period basis, or applied to a negative tax transfer. The child support transfer would automatically cease with unemployment of the absent father, though it is possible that a portion of any disability or unemployment compensation benefits for which the absent parent might be eligible could continue to be transferred to the custodial parent.

Although it is possible to design a child support enforcement system in a way which approximates the priorities of adequacy, equity, and responsibility while retaining the present income-maintenance programs, it becomes more complicated and in so doing makes the system even more cumbersome and entangled than it already is. Because of lack of coordination, cumulative implicit tax rates, and inconsistent eligibility requirements among the various income-maintenance programs we have presently, inequities abound. Any attempt to superimpose a uniform, equitable child support collection mechanism upon the present structure would be quite difficult, and our three priorities would be considerably weakened. While extensive reform of the income-maintenance and positive tax systems is in the planning-and-design stage, consideration should be given to the form which the child support component will take. So far, little official attention has been paid to this critical function.

As all income classes will have to be provided with support enforcement services in order to meet the goal of horizontal equity, the issue of cost-effectiveness of child support collection should become secondary. Since it is the constitutional responsibility of the federal government to set and promote equity in terms of income-redistribution and taxation goals, child support collection would naturally be a federal—not a state—responsibility, and variant and vague state child support laws would be bypassed in order to better meet the social goals of adequacy, equity, and the promotion of parental responsibility. Nonpayment of child support as a federal offense could be made equivalent to the nonpayment of one's income-tax debt, with high costs associated with evasion of the obligation.

Mandating that states strive to meet these goals would be a virtually impossible task. The mechanisms necessary to foster this kind of income redistribution across geographic jurisdictions are realistically only possible at the federal level, where computerized information-gathering and disseminating machinery is already being put in place to enforce the present child support laws, and will certainly need to be expanded with welfare reform along the lines that Congress is now considering.

The Role of the Courts

A federal system of child support enforcement such as the one being proposed would significantly reduce the income-transfer role which is presently within the purview of family courts. Because the amount of support awarded in divorce cases is so closely linked with a judgment of relative guilt in regard to the grounds for the divorce, as Max Rheinstein has pointed out in *Marital Stability, Divorce, and the Law,*[19] such a system would likely contribute to the separation of support issues from decisions about whether or not conditions for granting a divorce have been met or custody determination. Thus the role of the courts would be restricted to issues such as paternity determination, marital dissolution, and the resolution of custody disputes. The cases involving child support evasion, like those involving income-tax evasion, would fall under the jurisdiction of the federal courts, with similar penalties for adjudicated guilt.

It is quite likely that increased child support enforcement efforts, especially those that cut across income classes, will serve to encourage an already accelerating incidence of custody petitions by fathers. It is also likely that noncustodial parents will demand more liberal visitation rights in return for the loss of much of their freedom to avoid paying adequate and equitable support. These issues will be discussed in greater detail below. Suffice it to say that if a system of child support collection and distribution such as the one proposed here were to be adopted, it is probable that the family courts will find themselves with more time to devote to resolving the kind of issues mentioned above—issues which are more clearly within the purview of these courts than are income-maintenance and redistribution functions.

The Role of the Office of Child Support Enforcement

The role of the Office of Child Support Enforcement would be changed substantially with complete federalization of collection and disbursement of child support. Services to establish that a support obligation does or does not exist would still need to be provided for that portion of the population for whom absent parents do not make voluntary declaration at their places of employment or local income-maintenance program office. Location and notification of the absent parent who has not made such a declaration, together with paternity investigation and determination services when such are necessary, would most likely remain as necessary and vital components of the program.

The Issues: Alimony and the Division of Property

The proposed system for withholding and dispensing child support payments is not original with this author. The Honorable Robert F. Drinan, priest, member of Congress, and former dean of the Boston College Law School, proposed as early as 1962 that such a withholding plan be adopted in order to insure children their fundamental right of support by their absent fathers.[20] At this time we might wish to expand that description to include their right to nurture and support by both parents. Although there are some, including judges of domestic relations or family courts, who cling firmly to a belief in the biological thesis that women are inherently suited to have responsibility for the care of children (especially during the "tender years"), many today are challenging that assumption.[21] A system such as the one proposed here would not have to reflect a position on the issue of which parent should be awarded custody, but would leave that area of dispute to the courts, within whose proper purview it falls.

On the other hand, there is no reason why a mother who is the absent parent should not be subject to the same support laws as a father who is the absent parent. On the contrary, the principle of horizontal equity requires that they be treated identically. However, given what we know about the favorable position of men in both the educational and occupational systems today, it is reasonable to suppose that women—especially those who have not been members of the labor force over a period of years—will be incapable in most instances of earning as much as their former spouses. This fact by itself does not release them from their obligation to help support their children if they have earnings or earnings capacity in excess of their own needs. The extent to which they would be required to contribute support should be based upon the same standard as that used to determine the extent of support required if the father is the parent who is absent from the home. (The issue of what the standard for support payments should be is the topic of the following chapter.)

We confront a problem, however, when it comes to the place of alimony and property settlements in the proposed system, for there is widespread disagreement as to the meaning and the function of alimony in marital dissolution. The most frequently cited definitions are:

1. Alimony as a continuation of the husband's duty to support his wife;
2. Alimony as "damages" for breach of the marital contract by the husband; and
3. Alimony as payment of a debt owed either for services rendered during the course of the marriage or for the former wife's contribution to the marriage.

Within these general limits, alimony can be temporary or permanent, and granted in a lump sum or periodic payment form.[22] Whether the state has community-property laws or not, there is a tendency for the distinction between alimony and child support to become blurred. Admittedly, there is no reasonable way to avoid inclusion of the needs of the custodial parent with those of the children when the amount of support awarded is in any way contingent upon the level of need of those children. In the words of one writer, "It is not possible to provide one standard of living for the children and another for the custodial parent."[23] However, it seems unreasonable to assume that alimony awarded for any of the above reasons (with the possible exception of damages awarded for breaking the marital contract) is actually available as part of the absent parent's share of child support. This would be equivalent to being credited twice. That is, if alimony is payment for matrimonial services rendered by the former wife, it shouldn't simultaneously serve as the absent parent's share of child support. Unfortunately, as appealing as this logic may be, the fact remains that unless child support collection and dispersal is separated from the issue of alimony, the boundary between the two will be apt to remain fuzzy in the court's mind. Therefore, it is proposed that the adjudication of alimony remain a function of the private sector. It might be more appropriate for such petitions to be presented as civil suits, to be heard in the appropriate civil courts, rather than as petitions presented in domestic relations, family, or circuit courts. Thus child support would be left uncontaminated by the alimony adjudication process.

Custody and Visitation

The history of custodial arrangements following marital dissolution has, as some believe, favored mothers. In one respect this is true. Women have been assumed by society in general and family courts in particular to be more nurturant than men, by virtue of their sex alone. Without contributing to that debate, an examination of the factual consequences of the practice of granting custody to mothers (unless lack of fitness to "mother" a child properly can be proven)[24] reveals that mothers end up bearing by far the greatest proportion of the economic burden of child-rearing. That one parent, whether mother or father, should bear both the greater personal and economic responsibilities for the children is intolerable by any standard of equity employed. At the very least, the parent who maintains the home for a child should be given credit for providing the routine care of a child—being on call much of the time, especially when the children are young, nursing a sick child, often having to take time off from a job and perhaps losing earnings as a consequence, in addition to doing the shopping, cooking, laundry, and so forth. Recognizing the value of this contribution would suggest that, all other things being equal, the noncustodial parent should meet the greater proportion of the economic needs of the child (to what extent will be discussed in the following chapter).

The question of visitation rights and their relationship to child support is one which has plagued the courts for some time. In essence, the argument is whether the two are interdependent or independent of one another. Though the courts have ruled both ways, in general they tend to use support as leverage against those custodial parents who may be unwilling to permit more liberal visitation by the noncustodial parent. The downward modifications in support which occasionally result in these situations usually stop short of termination of the support obligation. Although the courts are said to make such downward modifications only if they determine that the child's welfare will not be jeopardized as a consequence,[25] it is the opinion of the author that the use of economic support of a child as a weapon of social coercion constitutes judicial tyranny, especially as we have found support payments to be on the whole abysmally inadequate to begin with. The obligation to support one's child should be distinct from and independent of the responsibility for providing love and nurturance to that child in accord with arrangements deemed by the court to be in the best interests of the child. A custodial parent who refuses to cooperate with the court in the matter of visitation can be coerced or punished by means other than the deprivation of support. It is difficult to see how anyone could believe that any of these coercive tactics, however, can insure happy parent-child relationships.

Family Life: Some Behavioral Consequences of Universal Enforcement

Illegitimacy. It is difficult to know what effect, if any, vigorous enforcement of the support obligation would have on illegitimacy rates. In both the married and unmarried populations, some women would bear children who would not have done so under conditions of economic uncertainty, such as those that presently prevail. Similarly, increasing the certainty surrounding child support will raise the potential costs and therefore the risks of carelessness for some men, both married and unmarried. The net effect is unpredictable but more to the point is the larger question, that of economic responsibility for the child once it arrives. As by far the greatest acceleration in illegitimacy rates is occurring in the adolescent population, where keeping the child rather than allowing it to be adopted is gaining in popularity, the question of the culpability of the father is quite a serious one. Should the adolescent father's parents be held responsible for his share of the child's economic support until the father reaches the age of majority? Or should the state provide for the support of the child in the interim, regardless of the ability of both sets of grandparents to provide support for the young mother and child?

Abortion. To the extent that income security is increased by greater assurance that child support would be forthcoming, it is likely that the demand for abortion, all other things being equal, would decrease if a national child support enforcement and collection system were to be adopted by the federal government. However, the Supreme Court ruling in 1973 which declared that the decision to carry a pregnancy to term or to seek an abortion is a unilateral one which rests entirely with the pregnant woman has raised some doubts as to the validity of paternal support statutes.[26] If such a decision is in fact a woman's alone, it has been argued, then the father of a child cannot be required to support the child if his preference for an abortion is not given favor and the mother chooses instead to bear the child. As he is not directly responsible for the birth, he bears no responsibility for support, which then must rest solely with the mother. On the other hand, a mother's passive act of not getting an abortion, while it might weaken the connection between sexual intercourse and birth, does not break it entirely. The father's role in the process might be diminished but it is not abolished altogether.[27] While this issue has yet to be resolved, a related one—the economic responsibility of both parents when neither wish for the child to be born—has been opened up by the most recent

Supreme Court ruling, to the effect that federal money cannot be used to provide voluntary abortions for which there is no medical justification.[28] If the state effectively eliminates abortion as an option for an indigent pregnant woman, does that not in fact negate the parental support obligation for both her and the child's father?

Conclusion

The above are but a few of the many issues posed by mandatory enforcement and collection of the child support obligation. By no means is this intended to be a complete listing or a comprehensive discussion of the issues. This chapter is intended to encourage exploration of structural alternatives to the present system of child support enforcement—a system which is wholly inadequate, unreliable, and inequitable.

Notes

1. If child support payments are taxed at a high rate, as are earnings, AFDC recipients who would be rendered ineligible for benefits if support payments were forthcoming, and who would consequently lose valuable benefits in kind such as Medicaid, would have little economic reason to pursue child support from the fathers of their children if these payments were not large enough to exceed the cash value of their total transfer losses. One would expect this effect to be more pronounced the narrower the difference between the state's payment and budgeted need, being greatest in states paying 100 percent of the budgeted need. For a lengthier discussion of notch effects and cumulative implicit tax—or benefit reduction-rates—see Michael C. Barth, George J. Carcagno, John L. Palmer, *Toward an Effective Income Support System: Problems, Prospects, and Choices,* Institute for Research on Poverty, The University of Wisconsin: Madison, Wisconsin, 1974, pp. 22-34, 101-102.

2. *Detailed Summary of Findings: Absent Parent Child Support Cost-Benefit Analysis,* Arthur Young and Company, Contract No. SRS-74-56: December 1975, p. 59.

3. Robert Hampton, "Marital Disruption: Some Social and Economic Consequences" *Five Thousand American Families—Patterns of Economic Progress*; Edited by Greg J. Duncan and James N. Morgan, vol. III, University of Michigan, Institute For Social Research, Survey Research Center: Ann Arbor, Michigan, 1975, p. 169. See also Heather L. Ross and Isabel V. Sawhill, *Time of Transition: The Growth of Families Headed by Women,* The Urban Institute: Washington, D.C., 1975, p. 25.

4. *Detailed Summary of Findings,* op. cit., p. 59.

5. *Policies and Procedures Manual* Texas Department of Public Welfare: Child Support Handbook, November 1975, Section 2130.

6. Patricia Moore, "Why Our Child-Support System Fails," Chicago *Daily News:* June 28, 1973.

7. Patricia Moore, "Why Lawyers Balk at Taking Cases Involving Child Support," Chicago *Daily News:* June 29, 1973.

8. Susan Sewell, *Compliance With Child Support Obligations,* individual research under the direction of Professor John J. Sampson, The University of Texas School of Law: May, 1976, pp. 15-16. By permission of the author.

9. Ibid., pp. 16-17 and Appendices V-IX.

10. John J. Sampson, *Theory and Trends in Child Support Law,* course materials prepared at the University of Texas School of Law, Austin, Texas 1977.

11. Sewell, op. cit., p. 18.

12. *Wage Garnishment, Attachment and Assignment, and Establishment of Paternity,* background information prepared by the staff for the Committee on Finance, United States Senate, U.S. Government Printing Office: Washington, D.C., October 1975, pp. 15-50.

13. Betty Spaulding, *Child Support and the Work Bonus,* testimony at the hearing on S. 1842, S. 2081, before the Committee on Finance, United States Senate, Ninety-third Congress, First Session: Washington, D.C., 1973, pp. 79-83.

14. *First Annual Report to the Congress on the Child Support Enforcement Program,* Office of Child Support Enforcement, Department of Health, Education and Welfare: June 30, 1976, p. 102.

15. Ibid., p. 103.

16. Ibid., p. 86.

17. Ibid. The mean cited here was calculated by adding third quarter F.Y. 1976 AFDC and non-AFDC collections from the tables on pages 121 and 129 and dividing by the number of successful actions taken during that same period, as reported on page 133.

18. Harold Watts, *Income Supports: Putting an Income Floor Under Every American Family,* working paper, Institute for Research on Poverty, University of Wisconsin: Summer 1976, p. 33.

19. Max Rheinstein, *Marital Stability, Divorce, and the Law,* The University of Chicago Press: Chicago, 1972, p. 380.

20. Robert F. Drinan, S.J., "The Rights of Children in Modern American Law," *The Rights of Children: Emergent Concepts In Law and Society,* ed. Albert E. Wilkerson, Temple University Press: Philadelphia, 1973, p. 43.

21. Joseph Goldstein, Anna Freud, and Albert J. Solnit, *Beyond the Best Interests of the Child,* Free Press: New York, 1973, pp. 38 and 132. See also Daniel Molinoff, "Life with Father," *The New York Times Magazine:* May 22, 1977, pp. 13-17.

22. Richard Constance, "Enforcement of Maintenance and Support Under

the Missouri Dissolution Act," The University of Missouri-Kansas City *Law Review,* Vol. 44, No. 3: Spring 1976, pp. 416-437. See also Homer Clark, *The Law of Domestic Relations in the United States,* Alimony and Property Divisions, Sections 14.1-14.12, West Publishing Co., St. Paul, Minn. 1968.

23. Isabel V. Sawhill, *Developing Normative Standards for Child Support and Alimony Payments,* revised draft, The Urban Institute: Washington, D.C., February 1977, p. 3. By permission of the author.

24. An important exception to this was a recent case in which a New York court granted custody to the father, not on the grounds that the mother was unfit, but that the father was deemed to have greater fitness. See Molinoff, op. cit., pp. 14-15.

25. Noranne Stradley, "Family Law: Construing Ohio Revised Code 3109.05: Are the Right to Visitation and the Duty to Support Mutually Dependent?," *Capital University Law Review,* Vol. 3-4: 1974-1975, pp. 283-290.

26. Martin R. Levy and Elaine C. Duncan, "The Impact of Roe Versus Wade on Paternal Support Statutes: A Constitutional Analysis," *Family Law Quarterly,* Vol. X, No. 3: Fall 1976, pp. 179-201.

27. Ibid., p. 193.

28. Poelker v. Doe, Supreme Court 75-442, June 20, 1977.

7   What Should Be the Standard Measure of Ability to Pay?

Introduction

The preceding chapter implicitly assumed that national public enforcement of the parental support obligation through the machinery of the federal government would not only increase the reliability and regularity of support payments, but raise the level of that support as well. Though this does not necessarily follow, it is likely that it would. The factors that would determine whether or not the overall level of child support payments would rise include:

1. The proportion of those not presently receiving support who would, given fundamental change in the enforcement system along the lines suggested; and
2. The extent to which child support payments would be adjusted upwards to reflect more closely the absent parent's actual ability to pay support.

The first condition requires further investigation. Prior to estimating this proportion, we need to know what percentage of those eligible for support are not receiving it because of the relatively high real and personal costs of pursuing it through the present legal system. As mentioned in earlier chapters, these costs include both those directly attributable to the process itself and others, such as the fear of retribution—or even physical violence—perpetrated by the absent parent, concern that the absent parent will cease visiting the children, the costs associated with the expenditure of time and energy often diverted from more urgent or gratifying pursuits, and so forth.

In addition, some of those not presently receiving support may do so when collection is federalized, if federalization brings with it greater compliance. Greater compliance is contingent upon how far the federal government is willing to go to enforce the new law and the extent to which the new child support law is perceived to be just and equitable.

Much of the confidence in the inherent equity and justice of child support enforcement and collection will hinge upon the selection of the measure of ability to pay which will be the basis of child support standards. Consensus as to the principles which underlie this choice is a necessary condition to success of such a public endeavor.

The principles which the author proposes are as follows:

1. Children of divorced or never-married parents should have no less a claim on the economic resources of those parents than do children whose parents are married to one another;

2. Economic consideration is due the parent who has custody of a child, as a consequence of the time, energy, and personal sacrifice entailed in providing a home and primary care for that child;

3. Whenever possible, the economic claims of prior children should not be displaced by those of subsequent unions, this is perhaps the most sensitive issue of all of those related to child support enforcement policy, and one that we will discuss in later pages;

4. The child support payment itself should never be so high as to
   a. reduce the economic well-being of the paying parent to a point below that of the recipient family; nor should it
   b. reduce the economic well-being of the paying parent to a point where he or she is eligible for public assistance;

5. It is within the proper purview of the federal government to insure that all parents, regardless of income, race, social status, or geographic location, support their children in accordance with their ability to do so; and finally,

6. Child support payments should be based upon the goal of equalizing the relative economic well-being of the household in which the child resides and that of the absent parent.

In other words, policies which strive to meet the above criteria regarding child support standards and practices would help insure that children receive the full economic benefit of both parents' resources, regardless of family characteristics such as marital status, race, and so forth.

Before turning to a discussion of the form that a standard such as this might take, it could be useful to look at some implicit and explicit standards currently in use.

Current Standards for Child Support and Ability to Pay

The lack of a uniform standard for child support payments—one which is consistently employed by courts within a jurisdiction as well as between jurisdictions—was well documented in the early paragraphs of chapter 4. In that chapter we pointed out that this absence of uniformity was largely the consequence of the strictly protected tradition of judicial discretion in this country. This tradition has prevailed in the area of child support adjudication in spite of its basic conflict with the promotion of equity, a tradition that has enjoyed at least equal favor within the legislative/judicial sphere. In spite of this prevailing tradition, there have been a few persons within the law profession who have advocated uniform standards in preference to total judicial discretion, on the grounds that an emphasis upon promoting equity would engender more respect for the adjudication process and reduce the number of appeals that are due to a belief that judicial discretion was abused.[1] These arguments have great merit if respect for the adjudication process would lead to greater compliance with support orders, and if fewer appeals would free time for swifter initial adjudication.

Perhaps because of the strength of the judicial discretion tradition, a portion of the 1974 federal law (P.L. 93-143) which required the states to develop normative child support standards was later countermanded. These standards were to have been used primarily in an administrative fashion, to guide child support enforcement program personnel in securing voluntary agreements for the support of children. A later federal regulation to the effect that support had to be adjudicated or based on a legally enforceable agreement returned the bulk of child support enforcement to the courts, and thus to the tradition of judicial discretion.[2]

Prior to this time, however, many of the states did develop child support standards. To the extent that these standards reflect those that prevailed in the respective locales, a close look may reveal clues as to current perspectives on the topic of ability to pay. (For instance, according to the Massachusetts Child Support Enforcement Unit their formula for determining the amount of child support obligation followed closely the allowance generally determined by the Massachusetts court system.[3]) Toward this end, the standards for child support payments for seven states' child support enforcement programs were obtained and examined.

For the measure of the absent father's ability to pay, Georgia and Wisconsin used the Bureau of Labor Statistics' "moderate" cost-of-living standard for his family unit (this was about 50 percent higher than Social Security Administration poverty levels).[4] Iowa, Maine, Massachusetts, and Texas used net taxable earnings[5], and Tennessee used the state's need standard—the same one that was used to determine AFDC eligibility.[6] Five of the seven states proposed taking from 13 to 75 percent of the surplus as child support for the dependent family, with the implicit tax rate on the earnings of the absent parent increasing as income increased (more so in some states than in others, however). Tennessee proposed taking *all* of the amount which was in excess of the state's need standard, up to the need standard of the dependent family. The Wisconsin standard for child support payment was based upon a prorated share of the Bureau of Labor Statistics' need standard for the dependent children. These standards suffered from a lack of uniformity, but all made adjustments for the number of children for whom the child support was intended. Iowa stood alone in its disregard for the number of dependents in an absent father's current family unit. As such, it was the only one of the seven states surveyed that did not allow for an implicit shift in economic responsibility with an absent father's further reproduction, but based the standard for the amount of child support due the former family solely upon the number of children in that family and the absent father's income.

To the extent that all of these standards reflect the adjudicated support trends in those states, it is likely that discretion within the administrative-judicial enforcement system accounts for some of the unexplained variance in the predictive model tested in chapter 3. Future research should address this question directly, however.

All of these states, then, employed earned income as the underlying measure of ability to pay. The discrepancies between their standards arose at the points where standards of economic well-being were chosen against which to compare father's earnings in order to determine the amount of surplus which was available, and judgments were made as to how much of the surplus should go toward child support.

Others—journalists and social scientists—have implicitly or explicitly based the standard for child support upon the earnings of the father, the extent of his current family obligations, and the needs of the dependent family, though the priority ordering of these three factors changes from author to author. Alvin Schorr, for instance, implicitly suggested in his article "The Family Cycle and Income Development" that the needs of a man's second family came first in terms of the disposition of his income.[7] Though he asserted this out of concern that the enforcement of support for children of prior unions would cause economic hardship for the current family, such a view tends to foster an irresponsible attitude toward prior duties that are deemed to be presently inconvenient. On the other hand, those who focus upon the needs of the child support-dependent family as opposed to the availability of resources under the control of absent fathers have done so primarily out of concern for the extent of economic deprivation of some of these families, rather than for promoting equity for all support-eligible children. A researcher who reported that the average amounts of court-ordered support ranged from only $31 to $100 per child per month (only six courts were included in this sample and their locations were not reported) evaluated these sums explicitly in terms of the extent to which the needs of the dependent family were unmet by so little support.[8] As nothing was mentioned about the ability of the absent father to pay support, one can only surmise that this researcher believed that the support did not adequately reflect his ability to pay.

In spite of the fact that the authors cited above disagree as to the normative standards for child support payments, current earnings have been the prevailing measure of ability to pay. In no case has the measurement of wealth, either real or in the form of human capital, been suggested as a possible alternative measure of ability to pay. However, it is probable that measures of real wealth and human capital are indeed taken into account by the courts at the time support is set. The problem, then, may be not merely the inadequacy and absence of standards for the measurement of ability to pay, but that the standards used are largely implicit, highly variable, and lacking in uniformity. The result is inequity, irrationality, and, possibly, low compliance rates. Lack of confidence in the equity and rationality of child support standards quite likely contributes to low compliance with support orders.

Toward a More Adequate and Equitable Child Support Standard

In keeping with the normative principles presented earlier in this chapter, two proposals for a child support payment standard are introduced for discussion and evaluation. Though the basic formula is the same for each, the two differ from one another in that the first uses earned income alone as the underlying measure of economic well-being, while the second relies upon estimates of earnings capacity as the measure of an individual's relative economic position.

Earned Income and Child Support

At the present time most child support standards, whether implicit or explicit, are based upon the actual earnings of both parties.[9] Thus, the higher the absent parent's earnings, all other things being equal, the higher the child support. Conversely, the higher the custodial parent's earnings, the lower the support received. In fact, however, as we have already learned, the present system does not deliver support in so simple and clear-cut a fashion.

We are proposing for discussion and evaluation the application of a formula similar to that used in chapter 4, which would establish the amount of the child support transfer. Such a discussion is warranted by the extent and nature of the inequities and the general inadequacy of the present means for establishing the level of child support due a family. Modifications of the basic formula (see page 71) should be such that it remains simple to use and self-adjusting to yearly changes in federal poverty-level standards by family size and wage rates. In terms of adequacy, such a formula would put child support at the disposal of each dependent family in amounts that in most instances would greatly exceed those presently being transferred to them (see Table 7-1).

It will be recalled that two limits were placed upon the transfer procedure: that the income-poverty ratio of the absent parent not be reduced to a point less than that of the family in which the children live; or that no money be transferred at all if the absent parent's income-poverty ratio was less than unity, indicating income insufficient for meeting the needs of the current family. These two constraints are incontestably reasonable. In keeping with our priority of enforcing responsibility, we might consider modifying the latter limitation to the

Table 7-1

Average Amounts of Child Support Based Upon Eight Standards

Standard or Formula	Number	Average Amount of Child Support	Remaining Income or Welfare Deficit	Percent of Pre-transfer Female-Headed Families Removed From Poverty by Child Support
No Standard (the present system)	193	$ 538.83	$2,964.08	3 (N=6)
Income-Poverty Ratio Equalization	193	3,565.79	286.72	63 (N=122)
Welfare Ratio Equalization	188[a]	2,933.49	178.20	72 (N=136)
Ten Percent of Absent Father's Income in Excess of Need	193	446.68	3,004.34	2.6 (N=5)[b]
Twenty Percent of Absent Father's Income in Excess of Need	193	911.73	2,605.02	8 (N=15)[b]
Thirty Percent of Absent Father's Income in Excess of Need	193	1,367.41	2,205.69	11 (N=21)[b]
Forty Percent of Absent Father's Income in Excess of Need	193	1,823.09	1,806.37	14 (N=26)[b]
Fifty Percent of Absent Father's Income in Excess of Need	193	2,278.77	1,407.05	16 (N=26)[b]

[a]The number of observations used in this calculation is slightly less than the others because data which were essential for accurate estimation of earnings capacity were missing in five case records.

[b]Comparable figures based upon percentages of estimates of the absent fathers' earnings capacity are 6, 9, 12, 18, and 20 percent of female-headed families removed from poverty (also determined on the basis of earnings capacity).

extent that no less than one dollar be transferred per accounting period, primarily for symbolic reasons. As only nontransfer, taxable income from earnings, investments, inheritance, and so forth would be counted, absent parents whose disability benefits (or the like) placed them above the poverty threshold would also be required to contribute one dollar, unless program provisions such as dependents' allowances made greater transfers possible.

A special problem arises in the choice of family-unit rules for determining the value to be placed in each family denominator. In the event a custodial parent remarried, it would not be equitable to make a new spouse implicitly responsible for supporting the children of another union. Similarly, we would not want to reduce (perhaps to nothing) the absent parent's responsibility to the children of a former union when he or she acquired new responsibilities. This would be tantamount to the former family, or society, subsidizing a new family because, as newly acquired responsibilities increased, the amount transferred to the former family as child support would *decrease,* thus shifting a greater proportion of these earlier responsibilities to others. For a former wife or society to carry an increasing share of this responsibility as a consequence of the absent father's further reproduction is untenable. The situation would be complicated further if the subsequent spouses already had children by previous unions. Here we are presented with a particularly knotty problem, because the reduction of an absent parent's responsibility for a former family with the acquisition of additional dependents would serve to facilitate a shift of that responsibility to the custodial parent or society, which is precisely the effect reform should strive to abolish. On the other hand, to disregard the needs of subsequent children is also untenable.

In order to resolve this dilemma, beginning with a value position that favors original or earlier family obligations, a two-part solution is proposed. The first part would state explicitly that the amount of child support would be fixed at remarriage as a proportion of the absent parent's income. Thus, if the amount required to approximate the equalization of income-poverty ratios at the time of the last accounting period were, say, 27 percent of earnings in excess of needs, that percentage would be fixed in the event the absent parent remarried or had another child. The income of a new spouse would not be assumed available for the absent parent's children by a former marriage, nor would the needs of the new spouse be included in calculations. Similarly, a child born subsequently would not serve to reduce the extent of the absent parent's responsibility to the former family. If an absent parent had already assumed additional responsibilities by the time the program was implemented, these responsibilities would have to be considered when making the initial calculations for equalizing income-poverty ratios. Thereafter, however, the needs of additional family members could not be used to reduce the extent of the support obligation, as support would be fixed at the proportion of the absent parent's income at the time the initial determination was made.

The child support would continue to be somewhat self-adjusting as the absent parent's income rose owing to personal effort and/or inflationary adjustments in wage and salary scales. Thus there would be no incentives or disincentives for remarriage or natality, yet no way to avoid meeting responsibilities already incurred other than to diminish labor supply. This latter possibility would always exist—it even exists under the present system to some extent—but because of the strong attachment to the labor force evidenced by married, prime-age males in this country (the age group most affected by the proposed program) little diminution in labor supply would be expected.[10]

Conversely, female heads of families containing young children, whose labor supply is quite income-elastic, might be expected to cease working altogether at the time of remarriage if child support payments remain constant, owing to the likely increase in net family income.[11] This presents a special problem in terms of what adjustment, if any, should be made in the child support which the custodial parent receives after remarriage. On the one hand, we do not want to discourage remarriage on the part of the custodial parent by adopting policies which would result in a reduction in child support upon remarriage. Also it would be inequitable to assume that any part of the new spouse's income would be available for the support of children by a former marriage, especially if the new spouse is supporting children from his own former marriage. Furthermore, if a female head of a family chooses to quit working outside the home at the time of remarriage, should we not simply drop her needs and income from our calculations on the assumption that her husband would be providing for her?

Recall that earlier we proposed that economic consideration be given the custodial parent in the calculation of child support payments, as a consequence of the time, energy, and personal sacrifice entailed in providing a home and primary care for the children. Therefore, to be consistent and promote equity we should determine that whether or not a custodial parent continues to work after remarriage, the child support payment should not change but be fixed at the level established at the time of remarriage. In the event a nonworking custodial parent began working after child support had been fixed as a consequence of either party's remarriage, some reduction in child support payments made by the absent parent, consistent with incomes and total circumstances, would probably be indicated.

Although it is not within the limited purview of this chapter to propose specific solutions to the special problems that arise as a consequence of all changes in employment and marital status, the general guidelines of equalizing income-poverty ratios between absent parents' households and those in which their children live, and maintaining equity, are the main points of the proposal, and those intentions should prevail.

Earnings Capacity and Child Support

Essentially, a child support formula which utilizes estimates of earnings capacity instead of income as the basic measure of economic well-being would not change the manner in which the standard would be applied at all. However, when assuming that the human capital of all relevant adults would be fully employed in the labor market child support payments might tend to be lower than if they were based upon actual earnings. The average payment, it will be recalled, based upon our sample of splits from the Michigan Panel Survey, dropped by $632.

Using earnings capacity instead of income as the basic measure of economic well-being would also avoid many problems associated with labor supply. By assuming earnings of a particular level, given the individual's demographic characteristics, the formula might have a positive effect upon the labor supply of all the adults involved. That is, the child support would not be reduced in the event the custodial parent had actual earnings in excess of his or her estimated earnings capacity, nor would the absent parent's contribution be increased if his or her actual earnings exceeded the estimated earnings capacity. Furthermore, insofar as estimates of earnings capacity incorporate demographic measures such as race and geographic location, child support payments so derived will be responsive to different unemployment rates for certain classes of individuals.

Child support standards based upon estimates of earnings capacity might be more acceptable to the public than standards based upon actual earnings. The basic formula which we are suggesting represents a dramatic change in the way people usually think about child support payments. As child support based upon earnings capacity rather than actual earnings would reduce the effective "bite" which is put upon noncustodial parents, such a formula might be more acceptable to this group than one based upon actual earnings. More than this, however, the promotion of equitable sharing of the responsibility for the children of a union demands that economic expectations be incorporated in a child support standard. The use of estimates of earnings capacity as the basic measure of economic well-being might be one way of doing this.

Other Alternatives

Though falling short of some of the normative specifications which we earlier laid out, a child support formula based upon a percentage of the absent parent's earned income is introduced at this point, primarily for comparative purposes.

Given that the cost of raising two children to the age of eighteen in a middle-income, two-child family was estimated by one researcher to have been $61,443 in 1972 (an average of $5,120 per year),[12] Table 7-1 suggests that more than half of an absent parent's excess income (income in excess of current needs) would have to be transferred as child support just to meet half of the needs of two children!

It becomes clear than that child support standards that would come close to equalizing the economic burden of child-rearing after family dissolution would require implicit tax rates on the absent parent's income that would often approach and occasionally exceed 50 percent. If we were to add an amount for compensation to the custodial parent for the provision of primary care for the child or children, the amount of child support would certainly approach or exceed half of the absent parent's earnings in excess of needs in many instances. That this approach to setting levels of child support would represent a fundamental shift in public thinking and policy cannot be denied. Though many would view this shift as one that is long overdue, its political feasibility is highly questionable at this point in time.

Summary

The greatest drawback of the income-based formula is the difficulty reducing some of the behavioral consequences which the use of such a formula would encourage. Labor supply would most certainly be affected in the ways described, as would family formation and composition, if built-in controls such as the ones described were not designed. Such controls would no doubt be subject to constitutional tests and, perhaps more seriously, to ethical and practical inquiry.

Fixing child support payments at one time in order to prevent a shifting of parental economic responsibility might give rise to other inequities with the passage of time and changes in individual circumstances. Child support standards built upon estimates of earnings capacity, on the other hand, would penalize those whose actual earnings were substantially lower than their earnings capacity, while those with earnings greater than their earnings capacity might not be paying their full share of support in relation to their real ability to do so. This brings us back once again to the fundamental question of which is the better measure of economic well-being. Until a fuller exploration of alternative measures of economic well-being is available, it may be that political features alone warrant giving preference to actual earnings over estimates of earnings capacity as the preferred basis for designing a formula for setting child support payment levels.

The adoption of any of the above bases for developing child support standards would necessitate dealing with problems encountered at the interface of the positive tax system and the income-maintenance system. As both of these are presently pending reform, precise suggestions as to how child support transfers would fit into the overall scheme are impossible. Assuming, however, that the welfare-reform proposals of the Carter Administration are implemented in the same general form as those before Congress, that the earned-income tax credit will be extended to some middle-income families, and that moderate-income workers will be granted more positive tax breaks in coming months, we can make some suggestions about child support reform.

Although the Carter welfare-reform plan would provide cash assistance to intact families whose able-bodied heads have earnings insufficient to meet the family's minimal needs, and thus reduce the incentives for family dissolution that are in the present AFDC program, it appears impossible to abolish those incentives altogether.[13] Because there will still be incentives for some families to split up to take advantage of certain features of the proposed guaranteed-income program, policies which would make the noncustodial parent automatically subject to a child support deduction when he or she became subject to positive taxes might help keep some families together or encourage reconciliations. At the very least, a responsible attitude toward the former family would be encouraged by the automatic deduction of child support from wages.

As the Carter Administration moves in the direction of a guaranteed family income or negative-income transfer program, more extensive mechanization is almost a certainty. A logical step toward some sort of centralized income-accounting system would be the combination of the parent-locater and income-maintenance computer systems. Decisions remaining to be made will include those surrounding the topic of this chapter—the choice of a standard measure of ability to pay, and a formula for determining the level of child support based upon that measure.

In addition, the judicial sector would be required to forfeit its discretion in the matter of setting child support levels unless exceptions to the application of the standard are being sought. Harold Watts has suggested that paternity be declared and publically registered at birth of a child, and as with the mandatory child support deduction, subject only to appeal by the designated father or absent parent.[14] Thus the burden of proof of nonpaternity would fall on the absent parent. The courts would retain their jurisdiction in cases in which paternity is disputed, though not in setting the amount of support to be paid. The question of whether to require the cooperation of the mother in the identification and location of the father of a child as a condition of eligibility for public transfers should await the findings of future research of the type suggested earlier. Among other things, this research should examine the relationship between various levels of cooperation and different benefit reduction or implicit tax rates. It seems logical to suppose that as the implicit tax on child support drops, allowing the family to keep more of their AFDC grant, cooperation with location and enforcement efforts would increase.

In summary, an objective reevaluation of the implicit and explicit assumptions about the quality and quantity of child support payments—who pays and on what measures of ability to pay these payments are based—is most definitely appropriate. It certainly appears that child support payments have been set from a "minimal" point of view. Absent parents, generally speaking, want to pay as little as possible. The courts' concern with noncompliance, which they believe occurs when support orders are too generous, forces them into a compromising position that probably results in most support payments being set far lower than the absent parent's true ability to pay would suggest. The custodial parent quickly becomes complacent, feeling lucky to get anything at all if it comes regularly, is willingly given, and does not interfere with the quality of the absent parent's relationship with the children. In addition, the distinction between alimony and child support has tended to become blurred.[15] Taking the child support collection and dispersal function out of the courts would contribute to the demise of this dilemma. The next step would be the development of a national child support formula or standard, one that would be based as nearly as possible, we hope, upon the principles set forth and discussed in this chapter. By no means has this discussion been able to cover or resolve all of the issues related to the development of such a standard. At the very least, however, it should provoke further, much-needed inquiry into the subject.

Notes

1. Kenneth R. White and R. Thomas Stone, Jr., "A Study of Alimony and Child Support Rulings with Some Recommendations," *Family Law Quarterly,* Vol. X, No. 1: Spring 1976, p. 84.

2. "Support Obligations," 45CFR, 302.50, (a) 1 and 2, June 26, 1975.

3. "Formula for Determining the Amount of Support Obligation," *State Plan for Child Support Collection and Establishment of Paternity Under Title IV-D of the Social Security Act,* Massachusetts Department of Public Welfare: June 1975, Attachment 2.3A.

4. "Determination of Support Obligation," correspondence with Tracy Teal, Chief, Child Support Recovery Unit, Georgia Department of Human Resources: Atlanta, Georgia, December 1975. Also,

"Support Payment Formula," *State Plan Under Title IV-D of the Social Security Act,* Wisconsin Bureau of Child Support, Division of Family Services, Department of Health and Social Services: Madison, Wisconsin, December 1975, Attachment 2.3A.

5. "Formula for Determining Amount of Support Obligation," *Employee's Manual,* Child Support Recovery Unit, Iowa Department of Social Services: Des Moines, Iowa, revised September 1975, V-8-38.

"Formula for Determining Amount of Support Obligation," *State Plan Under Title IV-D of the Social Security Act,* Support Enforcement and Location Unit, Maine State Department of Health and Welfare: September 1975, Attachment 2.3A.

"Formula for Determining the Amount of Support Obligation," Massachusetts, op. cit.

"Schedule of Child Support Payments Based on Gross Earnings Less Federal Income Tax and FICA Withheld," CSH Manual, Texas Department of Public Welfare, November 1975, Appendix 1.

6. "Formula for Determining the Amount of Support Obligation," *State Plan Under Title IV-D of the Social Security Act,* Office of Child Support Services, State of Tennessee Department of Human Services: Nashville, Tennessee, June 1975, Attachment 2.3A, pp. 1-3.

7. Alvin Schorr, "The Family Cycle and Income Development," *The Social Security Bulletin:* February 1966, p. 24.

8. Betty L. Osburne, "Your Child's Keeper," *Phi Kappa Phi Journal,* Vol. 55, No. 3: Summer 1975, pp. 19-21.

9. Some might argue this point on the grounds that though actual earnings of the absent parent are used in determining the level of child support, presumptions are made about how much the custodial parent could make, in the event she is not currently employed outside the home. This, some say, results in payments being set lower, which forces many female heads of families to enter the labor force when they would not otherwise do so.

10. Irwin Garfinkel and Stanley Masters, *The Effect on Non-Employment Income and Wage Rates on the Labor Supply of Prime Age and Older Males,* Institute for Research on Poverty Discussion Paper no. 193-74, University of Wisconsin: Madison, 1974, p. 75.

11. Irwin Garfinkel and Stanley Masters, *The Effect on Non-Employment Income and Wage Rates on the Labor Supply of Prime Age Women,* Institute for Research on Poverty Discussion Paper no. 203-74, University of Wisconsin: Madison, 1974, p. 55.

12. Thomas J. Espanshade, *The Cost of Children in the Urban United States,* Greenwood Press: Westport, Connecticut, 1973, p. 80.

13. Katharine Bradbury et al., *The Effects of Welfare Reform Alternatives on the Family,* Institute for Research on Poverty, The University of Wisconsin: Madison, Wisconsin, June 1977, pp. 27-39.

14. Harold Watts, *Income Supports: Putting an Income Floor Under Every American Family,* unpublished paper prepared at the Institute for Research on Poverty, The University of Wisconsin: 1976, pp. 36-37.

15. This is a point at which this author finds herself at slight variance with another researcher who has tackled the problem of normative standards for child support. Isabel Sawhill of the Urban Institute believes that alimony, as an adjustment for the long-term opportunity costs of retiring from the labor force during marriage and childrearing, should be included in the post-divorce support payment, and that this portion should be continued after the child support portion ceases with youngest child's eighteenth birthday. *Developing Normative Standards for Child Support and Alimony Payments,* The Urban Institute: Washington, D.C., February 1977, pp. 16-21. This author's view is that inclusion of the custodial parent's needs in the calculation is a separate issue from that of alimony, and should be dealt with as suggested earlier. Above and beyond alimony, if any, inclusion of the caretaker's needs in our child support formula reflects to a very limited extent recognition of his or her continuing contribution to the welfare of the children.

8 Adequacy, Equity, and Responsibility: A Summary

In earlier chapters of this book we have seen that the present child support enforcement system has the result of imposing most of the costs, both real and personal, of family dissolution on the female-headed family. A glance at Table 4-1 confirms what the general public knows already—that most child support payments are so low, if they exist at all, as to require supplementation from some other source. Indeed, "supplementation" is hardly the correct term. Child support payments are seldom found to be the primary source of income for the recipient family. Our own data suggest that in the aggregate, mothers' earnings are the primary source of income, followed by public transfer payments as the secondary source, with child support ranking a poor third place. Had our subsample from the Michigan Survey on Income Dynamics been more representative of the population as a whole, we would probably have had a larger proportion of poor, female-headed families. Then the ranking of source of support for these families more likely would have been public transfers, earnings of the female head, and finally child support payments. Together with the fact that the custodial parent—usually the mother—must provide the children with the bulk of nurturance, supervision, care-taking, transportation, recreation, and so forth during sickness and health of all parties, it is clear which parent carries the disproportionate share of the cost of family dissolution in most cases. That this solitary burden extends for an average of five or six years, until remarriage or the youngest child reaches the age of majority, only compounds the inequities.[1]

The present system offers few incentives for and imposes enormous costs upon a parent who is granted custody of the children when a union fails or when a marriage fails to eventuate. On the other hand, the personal and economic costs to the absent parent of that failure are too often minimal. In fact, to the extent that his responsibility can be shifted to the mother and/or the public, there may be a positive incentive for him to leave his spouse and children, even if, and perhaps because, he cares very much for their economic well-being.[2] Although the exact shape of welfare reform is unknown at this time, it does appear that features which encourage family dissolution and parental irresponsibility are unavoidable without the disincentives afforded by vigorous child support enforcement. All other things being equal, a family should not benefit economically from dissolution. Under the proposed system, which provides fewer transfers to the intact family than to family members maintaining separate households, and a great many cash and benefits in kind to the fatherless family,[3] a vigorously and

135

successfully pursued system of child support enforcement may contribute to family dissolution in that it adds to total well-being. The magnitude of this effect would be contingent upon the extent to which females could be induced to dissolve unions by a social guarantee of child support, which would increase their net incomes. This effect might be modified, however, if child support payments offset the transfer payment at a high rate. The present welfare reform proposal before Congress calls for a reduction of eighty cents in transfer benefits for every dollar received in child support payments.[4]

On the other hand, increasing the benefits of dissolution to the custodial parent by guaranteeing the payment of equitable levels of child support increases the costs of dissolution from the absent parent's point of view. If these costs are greater than the costs of maintaining an intact family (or getting married if the pregnancy is illegitimate), a reduction in family dissolution and an increase in family formation could be expected to the extent that men are the initiators of such. This effect would cut across income classes, and is the one which the author believes would be most likely to dominate. This opinion is based on the recognition that sexual bias pervades society, resulting in women being awarded custody and conservatorship with far greater frequency than men; greater educational, occupational, and financial opportunities for men; and a wider range of sexual and social opportunities for men than for women. Because of these cumulative economic inequities, it is difficult to believe that in general women are the primary initiators of marital dissolution, in spite of the frequency with which they initiate divorce litigation.

The actual net effect of child support enforcement on dissolution rates, produced by the positive effect when women are the initiators of dissolution and the negative effect when men are the initiators, is unpredictable because we have no way of knowing the extent to which anticipated child support presently enters into a decision about marital dissolution. Assuming only that most of the present inequities are known, as would be their removal by substantial reform, the above effects for men and women can be anticipated. Though the net effect and its magnitude cannot be predicted with certainty, it is in keeping with our general goals of promoting equity and responsibility after marital dissolution that we have proposed a reevaluation of both the child support enforcement system as we know it today and the traditional, minimizing approach to setting child support payment levels.

The issue of promotion of responsible behavior in relation to reproduction, or natality, is a more complex issue and more difficult to predict. It is likely that the present child support enforcement system has an antireproductive effect only upon those men who are not very mobile, who are attached to jobs and social groups that discourage neglect of one's responsibilities, and who regard very seriously their duty to provide the most amenities possible for their children, regardless of the quality of their relationship with the former spouse. For all others, however, the present system has little, if any, antinatal effect. As a sense of responsibility entails economic and personal costs, a decision to have another child should not be made lightly.[5] This is precisely the foresight one would hope to encourage with a mandatory child support program. It is unlikely that the present system, which allows 79 percent of the absent fathers in our sample to avoid the child support obligation altogether, encourages much thought as to the consequences of reproduction. With each additional child a greater proportion of the responsibility for former children can be shifted to the mother and/or the state. This is not only inequitable, as mothers cannot shift the costs of their further reproduction to fathers of earlier children, but such irresponsible behavior can impose costs on the rest of society as well.

Policymakers who wish to arrest this effective shift in responsibility and also discourage the further reproduction of absent fathers can fix child support at a given level or percentage of income, as we have earlier suggested. However, to the extent that reproduction is not economically rational, they must be prepared to subsidize the subsequent children of an absent father whose net income after child support payments is insufficient to meet the needs of his new family. This is perhaps one of the most difficult inequities with which policymakers must deal, for it appears to be tantamount to choosing which children are to be given preference over which others when enforcing a claim to the father's income. At the very least, policymakers must decide which family the public should be prepared to subsidize. Consistent with the values made explicit at the beginning of the previous chapter, we feel priority should be given to earlier families in regard to the father's income, and society should subsidize subsequent families, if necessary.

The third issue—that of the family relationships—flows naturally out of the above discussion. It is quite possible that, as we interpreted some of our results from chapter 3, an absent father might view the payment of child support as entitlement to the right of meaningful involvement in his child's life. Therefore, the larger the child support, the greater his efforts to exercise his paternal rights and responsibilities.[6] Also, we would expect that a father making a larger contribution to his child's life would be anxious to remain in fairly close proximity to the child and thus more easily collect the rewards (e.g., the child's love and affection) of his investment.

There are of course opposing views. The traditional social casework view is that social workers should not encourage a woman to take legal action against a father for support of their child, on the grounds that it discourages reconciliation. Rapidly rising separation, divorce, and illegitimacy rates, coupled with appallingly low child support payments (when they exist at all) and little evidence of reconciliation, have cast doubts on this traditional view. We are now forced to reassess this implicitly male-centered perspective and look toward policies that foster, rather than ignore, parental responsibility. A federal program of child support enforcement and collection could be designed in such a way as to minimize adversary aspects of this function.

There remain a number of questions for which we still need answers. Most of these surround the measurement of the absent father's ability to pay support vis-à-vis the need of the dependent family. In particular, what is the maximum reasonable amount of support that we could demand from the absent father before collection would become virtually impossible? And should actual earned income or some other measure, such as wealth or estimates of earnings capacity, be used as the basic measure of ability to pay? The answers to these and other questions are necessary in order that we might develop an equitable and enforceable child support payment standard and the appropriate machinery for payment collection.

In the final analysis, the justification for expanding federal involvement in support enforcement efforts must be made in terms of securing the right of children to enjoy the fullest possible benefits to be derived from the resources of *both* parents. Maximum exploitation of the real and personal resources of custodial parents has in most cases already been realized. That fostering a more equitable sharing of this personal responsibility is within the purview of government is most certainly true, as is the encouragement of behavior consistent with a notion of social responsibility.

Notes

1. Heather L. Ross and Isabel V. Sawhill, *Time of Transition: The Growth of Families Headed by Women,* The Urban Institute: Washington, D.C., 1975, p. 25.

2. Ibid., pp. 109-112.

3. Sheldon Danziger, Robert Haveman, and Eugene Smolensky, *Welfare Reform Carter Style—A Guide and a Critique,* prepared for the U.S. Congress Joint Economic Committee, The University of Wisconsin-Madison: October 1977, pp. 23-31.

4. "Administration's Welfare Reform Bill," *Congressional Record,* HR-9030: September 12, 1977, Sec. 2106(A), p. H9285.

5. Glen G. Cain, *The Effect of Income Maintenance Laws on Fertility in the United States,* Institute for Research on Poverty Discussion Paper No. 117-72, University of Wisconsin: 1972, p. 1.

6. Although I am aware of no effort to do so, I would expect that an empirical-examination of the child support payments made by members of Fathers for Equal Rights, a social action group, would reveal payment levels and compliance rates far in excess of the average. On the other hand, to the extent that payments are used as leverage to force greater sharing of custody and more liberal visitation privileges, payments made by members of this group could be significantly less than those made by other, demographically comparable, absent fathers.

Appendix

Table A-1
Michigan Survey Subsample Category by Various Socioeconomic Characteristics

			Michigan Survey Subsample Categories	
			Family Splits in Years 1968-1974	
SES Characteristic	Female Heads in 1968	Former Members of Original Sample Families Setting Up Own Households as Female Heads in Years 1968-1974	With Record of Absent Spouse	Without Record of Absent Spouse
Race				
White	53	34	49	57
Minority	168	130	26	61
Mean Number of Children Eligible for Child Support	3.04	1.92	2.68	2.64
Percent of Female Heads With At Least One Illegitimate Child	45	62	0	0
Percent of Female Heads Remarried by 1974	22	20	27	19
Percent of Absent Fathers Remarried by 1974	–	–	35	–
Female Head Income	$3,176	$2,314	$4,767	$3,479
Absent Father Income	–	–	$10,327	$8,381
Modal Year of Split	1967	1972	1974	1974
Mean Child Support Including Those Receiving None	$213	$165	$1,053	$246
Mean Child Support for Those Receiving Any	$1,567	$1,125	$1,646	$1,611

Michigan Survey Subsample Categories

SES Characteristic	Female Heads in 1968	Former Members of Original Sample Families Setting Up Own Households as Female Heads in Years 1968-1974	Family Splits in Years 1968-1974	
			With Record of Absent Spouse	Without Record of Absent Spouse
Years of Education (Female Head)	10.46	10.90	11.69	11.23
Years of Education (Absent Father)	—	—	11.97	10.44
Age of Female Head at Time of Split	Mean 29.3 Median 28.5	25.8 20.7	31.7 30.0	28.8 26.9
Age of Youngest Child at Time of Split	2.24	3.60	6.21	4.48
Mean Welfare (Only for Those Who Receive it)	$2,079	$1,872	$1,327	$1,441
Mean Income of Female Head's New Husband	$10,779	$8,037	$11,775	$9,605
Mean Income of Female Heads in 1974 Who had Remarried by 1974	$2,458	$1,955	$3,475	$3,091
Percent of Female Heads with Illegitimate Child(ren)	44.8	61.6	0	0
Percent of Female Heads Receiving Transfers	45.2	54.3	22.7	33.1
Absent Spouse's Current Wife's Income	—	—	$5,038	0
Mean Income of Absent Fathers Who Remarried	—	—	$12,000	—
Total Number	221	164	75	118

Table A-2
Mean Child Support by Number of Years Since Split

Number of Years Since Split	Mean Child Support			
	All in Subsample	Number	Child Support Greater Than Zero	Number
1	$303.46	76	$1,281.28	18
2	415.83	48	1,247.50	16
3	430.20	51	1,828.33	12
4	288.83	58	1,675.20	10
5	493.92	65	1,689.74	19
6	262.05	39	1,703.33	6
7	194.46	26	1,685.33	3
8	625.00	2	1,461.00	1
9	190.10	59	1,246.22	9
10	221.43	28	3,100.00	2
11	303.69	32	1,388.29	7
12 or longer	188.83	94	1,044.12	17
Total[a]		578		120

[a]Unweighted subsample.

Table A-3
Contingency Table Analysis, Number of Years Since Split by Amount of Child Support

Sample Description	Number	X^2	Degrees of Freedom	Significance Level	Cramer's V	Contingency Coefficient
Including those with no support	578	135.75	132	.398	.146	.436
Excluding those with no support	120	133.64	121	.205	.318	.726

Table A-4

Regression Results for Combined Sample, White and Minorities

(Dependent Variable = Receipt/Non-Receipt of Child Support (Dummy))

Variable Name	Regression Coefficient	Standardized Regression Coefficient	Partial Correlation Coefficient	t-value with 549 df's	Partial F Value with 1 and 549 df's
1. Absent father's income	.000017	.1476	.125	2.9489	8.6959[c]
2. Female head's income	−.000005	−.0484	−.031	−.7333	.5377
3. Absent father's wife's income	.000012	.0280	.029	.6872	.4724
4. Female head's husband's income	−.000001	−.0159	−.017	−.4028	.1623
5. Number of years since split	.004647	.0533	.046	1.0757	1.1572
6. Female head's remarriage	−.144744	−.1461	−.144	−3.4157	11.6667[c]
7. Absent father's remarriage	.068684	.0290	.031	.7275	.5292
8. Absent father's education	−.007268	−.0327	−.030	−.7092	.50302
9. Female head's education	.009160	.0528	.047	1.1051	1.2213
10. Female head's occupation I	.064464	.0379	.029	.6763	.4573
11. Female head's occupation II	.031274	.0298	.022	.5221	.2726
12. Female head's occupation III	.053180	.0375	.034	.7935	.6297
13. Female head's occupation IV	−.002941	−.0029	−.003	−.0587	.0034
14. Absent father's occupation I	.053650	.0298	.026	.6072	.3687
15. Absent father's occupation II	.073750	.0340	.033	.7810	.6099
16. Absent father's occupation III	.054491	.0257	.025	.59514	.3542
17. Absent father's occupation IV	−.028940	−.0151	.014	−.3170	.1005
18. Absent father's residence	.198450	.0827	.078	1.8382	3.3789[a]
19. Absent father's retention	−.230558	−.2291	−.153	−3.6282	13.1637[c]
20. Non-South	−.049622	−.0598	−.061	−1.4259	2.0332

21. Race (white)	.202109	.2350	.207	4.9587	24.5888[c]
22. Welfare status	.004629	.0055	.004	.10091	.0102
23. Total amount of transfers	-.000014	-.0681	-.045	-1.0503	1.1031
24. Illegitimate status of children	-.009275	-.0109	-.010	-.2234	.0499
25. Number of children eligible for child support	.016222	.0661	.063	1.4721	2.1671
26. Age of youngest child at time of split	.000702	.0066	.006	.1381	.0191
27. Number of children in the current family of absent father	-.033546	-.0359	-.037	-.8728	.7617
28. Missing data (dummy)	-.245002	-.2849	-.146	-3.4476	11.8860[c]

Note:

$N = 578$

Multiple Correlation Coefficient = .4815

Coefficient of Determination = .2318

(Corrected = .1822)

[a]Significant at .10 level of significance.

[b]Significant at .05 level of significance.

[c]Significant at .01 level of significance.

Table A-5

Regression Results for Combined Sample, White and Minorities

(Dependent Variable = Total Amount of Child Support)

Variable Name	Regression Coefficient	Standardized Regression Coefficient	Partial Correlation Coefficient	t-value with 549 df's	Partial F Value with 1 and 549 df's
1. Absent father's income	.0487	.2179	.193	4.6206	21.3496[c]
2. Female head's income	−.0159	−.0733	−.050	−1.1783	1.3884
3. Absent father's wife's income	.0705	.0834	.092	2.1751	4.7311[b]
4. Female head's husband's income	−.0063	−.0417	−.048	−1.1245	1.2645
5. Number of years since split	2.4923	.0146	.013	.3116	.0971
6. Female head's remarriage	−292.3331	−.1501	−.157	−3.7256	13.8804[c]
7. Absent father's remarriage	489.4095	.1053	.119	2.7996	7.8376[c]
8. Absent father's education	31.8416	.0729	.071	1.6781	2.8159[a]
9. Female head's education	19.9547	.0585	.055	1.3003	1.6908
10. Female head's occupation I	141.0318	.0422	.034	.7990	.6385
11. Female head's occupation II	124.5024	.0605	.048	1.1225	1.2600
12. Female head's occupation III	108.0428	.0388	.037	.8707	.7581
13. Female head's occupation IV	64.2323	.0322	.030	.6922	.4791
14. Absent father's occupation I	312.9919	.0885	.081	1.913	3.6612[b]
15. Absent father's occupation II	−154.5679	−.0363	−.038	−.8840	.7815
16. Absent father's occupation III	354.3492	.0851	.089	2.0901	4.3687[b]
17. Absent father's occupation IV	192.6127	.0510	.049	1.1398	1.2990
18. Absent father's residence	385.2297	.0817	.082	1.9271	3.7137[b]
19. Absent father's retention	−406.0955	−.2054	−.146	−3.4513	11.9116[c]
20. Non-South	−52.4221	−.0321	−.035	−.8136	.6619
21. Race (white)	412.8224	.2443	.227	5.4701	29.9217[c]

22.	Welfare status	85.1229	.0512	.043	1.0022	1.0045
23.	Total amount of transfers	−.0295	−.0741	−.052	−1.2122	1.4694
24.	Illegitimate status of children	−23.6507	−.0141	−.013	−.3077	.0947
25.	Number of children eligible for child support	47.3899	.0982	.099	2.3226	5.3943[b]
26.	Age of youngest child at time of split	−7.1112	−.0339	−.032	−.7554	.5706
27.	Number of children in the current family of absent father	72.7319	.0396	.044	1.0219	1.0444
28.	Missing data (dummy)	−313.1769	−.1853	−.101	−2.3800	5.6646[c]

Note:

N = 578

Multiple Correlation Coefficient = .5589

Coefficient of Determination = .3124

(Corrected = .2773)

[a]Significant at .10 level of significance.
[b]Significant at .05 level of significance.
[c]Significant at .01 level of significance.

Table A-6

Regression Results for Combined Sample, White and Minorities

(Dependent Variable = Average (per child) Child Support Payment)

Variable Name	Regression Coefficient	Standardized Regression Coefficient	Partial Correlation Coefficient	t-value with 549 df's	Partial F Value with 1 and 549 df's
1. Absent father's income	.0190	.1361	.124	2.9362	8.6212[c]
2. Female head's income	.0026	.0190	.013	.3107	.0965
3. Absent father's wife's income	.0820	.1558	.174	4.1325	17.0778[c]
4. Female head's husband's income	−.0039	−.0419	−.049	−1.1496	1.3216
5. Number of years since split	4.2083	.0394	.037	.8590	.7378
6. Female head's remarriage	−102.8859	−.0848	−.091	−2.1409	4.5833[b]
7. Absent father's remarriage	323.1895	.1116	.128	3.0185	9.111[c]
8. Absent father's education	19.8949	.0731	.073	1.7119	2.9305[a]
9. Female head's education	9.3685	.0441	.043	.9967	.9935
10. Female head's occupation I	31.2482	.0150	.012	.2891	.0836
11. Female head's occupation II	36.5309	.0285	.023	.5378	.2892
12. Female head's occupation III	29.6040	.0171	.017	.3895	.1517
13. Female head's occupation IV	−23.8678	−.0192	−.018	−.4199	.1764
14. Absent father's occupation I	394.5046	.1789	.166	3.9376	15.5047[c]
15. Absent father's occupation II	81.8504	.0308	.033	.7643	.5842
16. Absent father's occupation III	142.5766	.0549	.059	1.3731	1.8854
17. Absent father's occupation IV	105.1393	.0447	.043	1.0158	1.0318
18. Absent father's residence	118.1092	.0402	.041	.9647	.9306
19. Absent father retention	−231.7554	−.1881	−.136	−3.2159	10.3417[c]
20. Non-South	−87.7712	−.0864	−.094	−2.2240	4.9462[b]
21. Race (white)	209.7380	.1991	.190	4.5375	20.5889[c]
22. Welfare status	5.8264	.0056	.005	.1120	.0125

23. Total amount of transfers	.0018	.0071	.005	.1185	.0141
24. Illegitimate status of children	−12.6810	−.0122	−.012	−.2695	.0727
25. Number of children eligible for child support	−20.9927	−.0698	−.072	−1.6798	2.8217[a]
26. Age of youngest child at time of split	2.9553	.0226	.022	.5125	.2627
27. Number of children in the current family of absent father	−18.5974	−.0162	−.018	−.4266	.1820
28. Missing data (dummy)	−166.5634	−.1582	−.088	−2.0667	4.2714[b]

Note:

N = 578

Multiple Correlation Coefficient = .5796

Coefficient of Determination = .3360

(Corrected = .3021)

[a]Significant at .10 level of significance.
[b]Significant at .05 level of significance.
[c]Significant at .01 level of significance.

Table A-7

Regression Results for Minorities Sample

(Dependent Variable = Receipt/Non-Receipt of Child Support (Dummy))

Variable Name	Regression Coefficient	Standardized Regression Coefficient	Partial Correlation Coefficient	t-value with 357 df's	Partial F Value with 1 and 357 df's
1. Absent father's income	.000031	.2391	.154	2.9463	8.6807[c]
2. Female head's income	-.000002	-.0221	-.014	-.2571	.0661
3. Absent father's wife's income	.000104	.1092	.096	1.8184	3.3065[a]
4. Female head's husband's income	.000018	.0113	.011	.2131	.0454
5. Number of years since split	.000801	.0120	.010	.1944	.0378
6. Female head's remarriage	-.034459	-.0378	-.037	-.6958	.4841
7. Absent father's remarriage	-.021199	-.0070	-.005	-.0941	.0089
8. Absent father's education	-.010255	-.0440	-.039	-.7344	.5393
9. Female head's education	.006982	.0481	.043	.8174	.6682
10. Female head's occupation I	.010791	.0056	.005	.0925	.0086
11. Female head's occupation II	.054967	.0575	.042	.7858	.6175
12. Female head's occupation III	-.001405	-.0013	-.001	-.0197	.0004
13. Female head's occupation IV	-.070423	-.0909	-.070	-1.3181	1.7375
14. Absent father's occupation I	-.547278	-.1225	-.116	-2.2006	4.8425[b]
15. Absent father's occupation II	.149628	.0664	.060	1.1328	1.2833
16. Absent father's occupation III	-.031387	-.0201	-.018	-.3359	.1129
17. Absent father's occupation IV	.006519	.0046	.003	.0596	.0036
18. Absent father's residence	.314884	.1309	.105	2.0009	4.0036[b]
19. Absent father retention	-.178291	-.2026	-.093	-1.7568	3.0864[a]
20. Non-South	-.040605	-.0628	-.058	-1.1029	1.2163
21. Welfare status	-.011469	-.0178	-.014	-.2693	.0725

22. Total amount of transfers	−.000014	−.0881	−.055	−1.0377	1.0769
23. Illegitimate status of children	−.013765	−.0213	−.018	−.3457	.1195
24. Number of children eligible for child support	.014373	.0804	.070	1.3339	1.7792
25. Age of youngest child at time of split	.003557	.0345	.030	.5633	.3173
26. Number of children in the current family of absent father	−.024181	−.0313	−.030	−.5577	.3110
27. Missing data (dummy)	−.234532	−.3053	−.122	−2.3291	5.4245[b]

Note:

N = 385

Multiple Correlation Coefficient = .4005

Coefficient of Determination = .1604

(Corrected = .0969)

[a]Significant at .10 level of significance.
[b]Significant at .05 level of significance.
[c]Significant at .01 level of significance.

Table A-8

Regression Results for Minorities Sample

(Dependent Variable = Total Amount of Child Support)

Variable Name	Regression Coefficient	Standardized Regression Coefficient	Partial Correlation Coefficient	t-value with 357 df's	Partial F value with 1 and 357 df's
1. Absent father's income	.0416	.2728	.175	3.3529	11.2416[c]
2. Female head's income	−.0119	−.0960	−.059	−1.1115	1.2355
3. Absent father's wife's income	.0940	.0851	.075	1.4133	1.9974
4. Female head's husband's income	−.0093	−.0517	−.051	−.9710	.9429
5. Number of years since split	−2.4127	−.0311	−.027	−.5018	.2518
6. Female head's remarriage	−67.2825	−.0634	−.062	−1.1644	1.3557
7. Absent father's remarriage	−344.2490	−.0976	−.069	−1.3092	1.7139
8. Absent father's education	−8.3575	−.0308	−.027	−.5130	.2631
9. Female head's education	8.2532	.0489	.044	.8282	.6859
10. Female head's occupation I	−17.3757	−.0077	−.007	−.1276	.0163
11. Female head's occupation II	121.6714	.1094	.079	1.4908	2.2224
12. Female head's occupation III	34.2141	.0266	.022	.4104	.1685
13. Female head's occupation IV	−46.4087	−.0515	−.039	−.7446	.5543
14. Absent father's occupation I	−486.1905	−.0935	−.088	−1.6755	2.8074[a]
15. Absent father's occupation II	174.7769	.0667	.060	1.1341	1.2862
16. Absent father's occupation III	109.7183	.0603	.053	1.0065	1.0130
17. Absent father's occupation IV	23.9382	.0145	.010	.18748	.0352
18. Absent father's residence	379.9524	.1358	.109	2.0693	4.2820[b]
19. Absent father retention	−141.9210	−.1386	−.063	−1.1986	1.4365
20. Non-South	−25.9939	−.0345	−.032	−.6051	.36617
21. Welfare status	24.4827	.0326	.026	.4928	.2428
22. Total amount of transfers	−.0213	−.1189	−.074	−1.3970	1.9517

23. Illegitimate status of children	-4.4219	-.0059	-.005	-.0952	.0091
24. Number of children eligible for child support	16.4237	.0789	.069	1.3063	1.7064
25. Age of youngest child at time of split	-1.5588	-.0130	-.011	-.2116	.0448
26. Number of children in the current family of absent father	19.9369	.0222	.021	.3941	.1553
27. Missing data (dummy)	-164.4063	-.1839	-.074	-1.3993	1.9581

Note:

N = 385

Multiple Correlation Coefficient = .3951

Coefficient of Determination = .1561

(Corrected = .0923)

[a]Significant at .10 level of significance.

[b]Significant at .05 level of significance.

[c]Significant at .01 level of significance.

Table A-9
Regression Results for Minorities Sample
(Dependent Variable = Average (per child) Child Support Payment)

Variable Name	Regression Coefficient	Standardized Regression Coefficient	Partial Correlation Coefficient	t-value with 357 df's	Partial F Value with 1 and 357 df's[a]
1. Absent father's income	.0134	.1537	.096	1.8272	3.3385[a]
2. Female head's income	−.0020	−.0286	−.017	−.3199	.1024
3. Absent father's wife's income	−.0023	−.0036	−.003	−.0576	.0033
4. Female head's husband's income	−.0032	−.0307	−.029	−.5571	.3104
5. Number of years since split	−1.4744	−.0333	−.027	−.5197	.2701
6. Female head's remarriage	7.1441	.0118	.011	.2096	.0439
7. Absent father's remarriage	−139.4260	−.0693	−.048	−.8987	.8077
8. Absent father's education	−3.9285	−.0254	−.022	−.4087	.0339
9. Female head's education	1.0820	.0112	.010	.1840	.1670
10. Female head's occupation I	−19.2547	−.0150	−.013	−.2396	.0574
11. Female head's occupation II	37.8813	.0597	.042	.7867	.6189
12. Female head's occupation III	−6.3183	−.0086	−.007	−.1285	.0165
13. Female head's occupation IV	−28.4917	−.0554	−.041	−.7747	.6001
14. Absent father's occupation I	−152.3263	−.0513	−.047	−.8898	.7917
15. Absent father's occupation II	265.5744	.1776	.153	2.9208	8.5313[c]
16. Absent father's occupation III	7.8414	.0076	.006	.1219	.0149
17. Absent father's occupation IV	−7.3110	−.0078	−.005	−.0971	.0094
18. Absent father's residence	51.6840	.0324	.025	.4771	.2276
19. Absent father retention	−33.3283	−.0570	−.025	−.4771	.2276
20. Non-South	−8.0793	−.0188	−.017	−.3188	.1016
21. Welfare status	−1.8478	−.0043	−.003	−.0630	.0039
22. Total amount of transfers	−.0099	−.0962	−.058	−1.0936	1.1959

155

23. Illegitimate status of children	-3.6379	-.0085	-.007	-.1327	.0176
24. Number of children eligible for child support	-5.4105	-.0456	-.039	-.7294	.5320
25. Age of youngest child at time of split	1.7878	.0261	.022	.4113	.1692
26. Number of children in the current family of absent father	-6.8575	-.0134	-.012	-.2298	.0528
27. Missing data (dummy)	-44.6001	-.0874	-.034	-.6434	.4140

Note:

N = 385

Multiple Correlation Coefficient = .3127

Coefficient of Determination = .0978

(Corrected = .0295)

[a]Significant at .10 level of significance.
[b]Significant at .05 level of significance.
[c]Significant at .01 level of significance.

Table A-10

Regression Results for White Sample

(Dependent Variable = Receipt/Non-Receipt of Child Support (dummy))

Variable Name	Regression Coefficient	Standardized Regression Coefficient	Partial Correlation Coefficient	t-value with 165 df's	Partial F Value with 1 and 165 df's
1. Absent father's income	.000015	.1487	.133	1.7300	2.9930[a]
2. Female head's income	−.000014	−.1244	−.080	−1.0305	1.0620
3. Absent father's wife's income	.000000	.0017	.002	.0222	.0005
4. Female head's husband's income	.000000	.0102	.010	.1340	.0180
5. Number of years since split	.021074	.1773	.132	1.7114	2.9288[a]
6. Female head's remarriage	−.302544	−.2955	−.272	−3.6362	13.2217[c]
7. Absent father's remarriage	.097656	.0509	.053	.6855	.4699
8. Absent father's education	−.003973	−.0200	−.018	−.2308	.0533
9. Female head's education	.004969	.0247	.019	.2450	.0600
10. Female head's occupation I	.150473	.1019	.066	.8480	.7192
11. Female head's occupation II	.037080	.0345	.024	.3084	.0951
12. Female head's occupation III	.190746	.1079	.097	1.2532	1.5705
13. Female head's occupation IV	.181200	.1347	.121	1.5634	2.4441
14. Absent father's occupation I	.090358	.0662	.055	.7018	.4925
15. Absent father's occupation II	−.045810	−.0236	−.022	−.2889	.0835
16. Absent father's occupation III	.290442	.0947	.094	1.2192	1.4864
17. Absent father's occupation IV	−.095364	−.0340	−.035	−.4536	.2057
18. Absent father's residence	.113269	.0515	.049	.6279	.3943
19. Absent father retention	−.241633	−.2261	−.171	−2.2243	4.9475[b]
20. Non-South	−.083800	−.0784	−.080	−1.0296	1.0601
21. Welfare status	.075689	.0563	.041	.5299	.2808

22. Total amount of transfers	−.000018	−.0539	−.038	−.4859	.2361
23. Illegitimate status of children	.088871	.0632	.058	.7457	.5560
24. Number of children eligible for child support	.009761	.0245	.024	.3114	.0970
25. Age of youngest child at time of split	−.004732	−.0441	−.038	−.4931	.2432
26. Number of children in the current family of absent father	−.027168	−.0260	−.025	−.3213	.1032
27. Missing data (dummy)	−.278367	−.2842	−.162	−2.1077	4.4425[b]

Note:

N = 193

Multiple Correlation Coefficient = .4861

Coefficient of Determination = .2363

(Corrected = .1113)

[a]Significant at .10 level of significance.
[b]Significant at .05 level of significance.
[c]Significant at .01 level of significance.

Table A-11

Regression Results for White Sample

(Dependent Variable = Total Amount of Child Support)

Variable Name	Regression Coefficient	Standardized Regression Coefficient	Partial Correlation Coefficient	t-value and 165 df's	Partial F Value with 1 and 65 df's
1. Absent father's income	.0538	.2210	.211	2.7688	7.663[c]
2. Female head's income	−.0231	−.0863	−.060	−.7704	.5935
3. Absent father's wife's income	.0737	.0971	.103	1.3271	1.7611
4. Female head's husband's income	−.0017	−.0126	−.014	−.1783	.0318
5. Number of years since split	11.6902	.0405	.033	.4209	.1771
6. Female head's remarriage	−684.4615	−.2752	−.273	−3.6472	13.3018[c]
7. Absent father's remarriage	726.7979	.1560	.173	2.2618	5.1156[b]
8. Absent father's education	61.8933	.1281	.123	1.5938	2.5402
9. Female head's education	24.6441	.0504	.042	.5386	.2901
10. Female head's occupation I	204.3365	.0569	.040	.5106	.2607
11. Female head's occupation II	122.0716	.0468	.035	.4501	.2026
12. Female head's occupation III	225.2576	.0525	.051	.6561	.4305
13. Female head's occupation IV	379.0487	.1160	.112	1.4499	2.1023
14. Absent father's occupation I	323.8326	.0977	.086	1.1150	1.2433
15. Absent father's occupation II	−374.4689	−.0793	−.081	−1.0451	1.0921
16. Absent father's occupation III	620.6986	.0833	.090	1.1551	1.3344
17. Absent father's occupation IV	−65.6528	−.0096	−.011	−.1384	.0192
18. Absent father's residence	287.6576	.0538	.055	.7070	.4999
19. Absent father retention	−540.0360	−.2080	−.169	−2.2040	4.8576[b]
20. Non-South	−116.9641	−.0451	−.050	−.6371	.4059
21. Welfare status	396.9071	.1214	.095	1.2320	1.5178
22. Total amount of transfers	−.0439	−.0542	−.041	−.5259	.2766

23. Illegitimate status of children	−25.7393	−.0075	−.007	−.0958	.0092
24. Number of children eligible for child support	152.4373	.1572	.166	2.1561	4.6488[b]
25. Age of youngest child at time of split	−22.9650	−.0882	−.082	−1.0611	1.1259
26. Number of children in the current family of absent father	222.2212	.0877	.090	1.1650	1.3573
27. Missing data (dummy)	−277.8618	−.1168	−.072	−.9328	.8701

Note:

N = 193

Multiple Correlation Coefficient = .5845

Coefficient of Determination = .3417

(Corrected = .2340)

[a]Significant at .10 level of significance.
[b]Significant at .05 level of significance.
[c]Significant at .01 level of significance.

Table A-12
Regression Results for White Sample
(Dependent Variable = Average (per child) Child Support Payment)

Variable Name	Regression Coefficient	Standardized Regression Coefficient	Partial Correlation Coefficient	t-value with 165 df's	Partial F Value with 1 and 165 df's
1. Absent father's income	.0233	.1498	.148	1.9239	3.7012[a]
2. Female head's income	−.0020	−.0116	−.008	−.1063	.0113
3. Absent father's wife's income	.0869	.1796	.192	2.5145	6.3227[c]
4. Female head's husband's income	−.0039	−.0451	−.051	−.6528	.4261
5. Number of years since split	17.5315	.0952	.079	1.0143	1.0288
6. Female head's remarriage	−259.0088	−.1633	−.170	−2.2179	4.9191[b]
7. Absent father's remarriage	457.9050	.1541	.176	2.2900	5.2440[b]
8. Absent father's education	28.4969	.0925	.091	1.1792	1.3906
9. Female head's education	19.3259	.0619	.053	.6787	.4607
10. Female head's occupation I	−3.3095	−.0014	−.001	−.0133	.0001
11. Female head's occupation II	34.6457	.0208	.016	.2053	.0422
12. Female head's occupation III	162.0810	.0592	.059	.7587	.5757
13. Female head's occupation IV	38.0054	.0182	.018	.2336	.0546
14. Absent father's occupation I	333.6681	.1579	.142	1.8463	3.4088[a]
15. Absent father's occupation II	−87.6958	−.0291	−.031	−.3933	.1547
16. Absent father's occupation III	363.8436	.0765	.084	1.0882	1.1841
17. Absent father's occupation IV	−57.3690	−.0132	−.015	−.1944	.0378
18. Absent father's residence	96.6640	.0284	.030	.3818	.1458
19. Absent father retention	−364.5041	−.2202	−.183	−2.3906	5.7151[b]
20. Non-South	−220.8866	−.1334	−.149	−1.9336	3.7387[b]
21. Welfare status	79.6747	.0382	.031	.3974	.1580
22. Total amount of transfers	−.0120	−.0232	−.018	−.2307	.0532

23. Illegitimate status of children	32.3633	.0149	.015	.1935	.0374
24. Number of children eligible for child support	−81.2570	−.1314	−.142	−1.8470	3.7387[a]
25. Age of youngest child at time of split	1.3278	.0080	.008	.0986	.0097
26. Number of children in the current family of absent father	4.5346	.0028	.003	.0382	.0015
27. Missing Data (dummy)	−252.8035	−.1666	−.106	1.3638	1.8599

Note:

N = 193

Multiple Correlation Coefficient = .6109

Coefficient of Determination = .3732

(Corrected = .2706)

[a]Significant at .10 level of significance.

[b]Significant at .05 level of significance.

[c]Significant at .01 level of significance.

Table A-13

1974 Social Security Administration Poverty Levels by Family Size (not including Alaska and Hawaii)

Family Size	Nonfarm Family	Farm Family
1	$2,800	$2,400
2	3,700	3,160
3	4,600	3,920
4	5,500	4,680
5	6,400	5,440
6	7,360	6,200

Source: *Federal Register,* Volume 41, No. 66, April 5, 1976, p. 14371.

Note: For family units with more than six members, add $900 for each additional member in a nonfarm family and $760 for each additional member in a farm family.

Table A-14

Distribution of Welfare Ratios (NEC) of Absent Fathers and Female Heads of Households in 1974[a]

Class	Class Intervals	Frequency		Percentage in Subsample	
		Female Heads	Absent Fathers	Female Heads	Absent Fathers
1	0-.49	90,000	0	4.09	0.0
2	0.5-.99	282,000	500	12.82	0.03
3	1.0-1.49	418,000	0	19.00	0.0
4	1.5-1.99	502,000	8,000	22.81	.36
5	2.0-2.49	129,500	27,000	5.89	1.23
6	2.5-100	779,000	2,165,000	35.40	98.39

[a]Total number = 2,200,500

Table A-15
Distribution of Comparative Welfare Ratios[a] **($NEC_{AF} - NEC_{FH}$)**

Class	Difference Intervals	Frequency	Percentage of Subsample Population
1	−1.49 to −1.00	30,000	1.30
2	−0.99 to −0.50	12,500	.54
3	−0.49 to −0.00	46,500	2.01
4	0.01 to 0.49	73,500	3.18
5	0.50 to 0.99	111,000	4.81
6	1.0 to 1.49	194,500	8.43
7	1.50 to 1.99	193,500	8.38
8	2.00 to 2.49	416,000	18.02
9	2.50 to 100	1,230,500	53.31

[a]Total number = 2,308,000

Table A-16
Child Support Unit Average Cost Per Case by Program Component — Five-County Average[a]

Component	Cost	
Intake	$ 2.34	
Location	113.00	(upper limit)
Financial Assessment	12.52	
Paternity	25.48	(4-county average)
Establishment of the support obligation	11.76	(direct costs *only,* as indirect costs are not estimated by the authors for this program component.)
Collection and enforcement	55.72	
Total	$220.82	

[a]Calculations are based on figures from *Detailed Summary of Findings: Absent Parent Child Support Cost-Benefit Analysis,* Arthur Young and Company: December 1975, pp. 37, 47, Exhibit 33, p. 54, Exhibit 42, and p. 71.

Table A-17
Child Support Collections Attributable to AFDC and Non-AFDC Caseloads

County	Collections		Caseload		Average Collections Per Case		Non-AFDC Caseload As Percent of Total Caseload	Non-AFDC Collections As Percent of Total Collections
	AFDC	Non-AFDC	AFDC	Non-AFDC	AFDC	Non-AFDC		
Orange	$3,406,159	$ 6,197,617	8,815	13,222	$395.48	$ 468.74	60	64
Sacramento	$2,831,123	$ 3,693,486	11,407	5,814	$248.19	$ 635.28	34	57
San Bernardino	$1,475,521	$ 2,533,222	5,476	7,652	$269.45	$ 331.05	58	63
Genesee	$4,710,134	$16,912,205	7,109	13,563	$662.56	$1,045.97	66	78
Seattle	$2,905,540	$ 1,210,656	8,878	1,270	$327.27	$ 953.27	13	29

Source: the Young Study, pages 15-19, Exhibits 5, 10, 11, 12, and 13.

Table A-18
Child Support Collections Regressed on Support Program Costs

Independent Variable	Regression Coefficient	Standard Error of Regression Coefficient	F-value	Significance Level
Child support enforcement costs	13.30	2.5	26.91	.000

Table A-19
Child Support Collections Regressed on Support Program Costs and State Dummy Variables

Independent Variables	Regression Coefficient	Standard Error of Regression Coefficient	F-value	Significance Level
Child support enforcement costs	4.864	2.9087	2.7960	.155
States				
Georgia	902883.79	543909.37	2.7556	.158
Iowa	144536.09	490566.78	.0868	.780
Maine	−64160.75	571195.13	.0126	.915
Massachusetts	749849.29	910558.37	.6782	.448
Oregon	163943.83	568698.22	.0831	.785
Tennessee	—	—	—	—

Table A-20
Child Support Collections Regressed on Support Program Costs, AFDC Expenditures, and State Dummy Variables

Independent Variables	Regression Coefficient	Standard Error of Regression Coefficient	F-value	Significance Level
AFDC expenditures	.0462	.0088	27.778	.006
Child support enforcement costs	5.2167	1.1557	20.375	.011
States				
Georgia	940253.00	215864.	18.973	.012
Iowa	−57957.28	198345.22	.085	.785
Maine	218981.41	232852.59	.884	.400
Massachusetts	−139547.02	544183.62	6.576	.062
Oregon	−134329.45	232570.87	.334	.594
Tennessee	—	—	—	—

Table A-21
Regression Equation for Child Support Determinants Model

$$Y = +B_1 X_1 + B_2 X_2 + \ldots + B_{21} X_{21} + e$$

where:

Y = child support, either receipt/nonreceipt, average amount per child, or total amount;

α = a "constant" representing the intercept of the regression line;

$B_1 - B_{21}$ = the slopes of the dependent variables on the respective independent variables, $X_1 - X_{21}$; that is, the statistical coefficients, or weights, for the variables $X_1 - X_{21}$;

X_3 = female head's nontransfer income from employment, investment, etc.;

X_4 = nontransfer income of current husband, if any, of female head;[a]

X_5 = number of years since the split;

X_6 = female head's remarriage status;

X_7 = absent father's remarriage status;

X_8 = absent father's educational attainment;

X_9 = female head's educational attainment;

X_{10} = female head's occupation;

X_{11} = absent father's occupation;

X_{12} = absent father's residence (same or different state than that of female head and their children);

X_{13} = absent father's mobility/stability;

X_{14} = female head's region of residence;

X_{15} = welfare status of female head;

X_{16} = total amount of public transfers to female head;

X_{17} = legitimate/illegitimate status of the child support-dependent children;

X_{18} = number of children of the female head for whom child support is expected;

X_{19} = age of the youngest child at the time of the split;

X_{20} = the number of children in the current family unit of the absent father;

X_{21} = missing data for some absent fathers; and

e = measurement error.

[a]Because a person enters our subsample only in the event she becomes a female head of household, we continue to refer to her in those terms even if she remarries.

Table A-22
Formula for Computing Gross Earnings Capacity

For all family units in our subsample, the estimate of GEC is as follows:

$$GEC_{fu} = \frac{EC_h \, (50 - W_{su})}{50} + \frac{EC_s \, (50 - W_{su})}{50} + Y$$

where

EC_h = head's imputed annual earnings capacity at 50 to 52 weeks of full-time work

EC_s = spouse's (if any) imputed annual earnings capacity at 50 to 52 weeks of full-time work

W_{su} = weeks sick or unemployed

Y = income from interest, dividends, rents, and miscellaneous other sources, not including government transfers, alimony, or child support.

Finally,

$$GWR_{fu} = \frac{GEC_{fu}}{PL}$$

Index

About the Author

Judith Cassetty graduated from George Peabody College for Teachers in Nashville, Tennessee and received the master's degree in social work from the University of Tennessee. She received the Ph.D. in social welfare from the University of Wisconsin-Madison, where she was affiliated with the Institute for Research on Poverty. Dr. Cassetty has worked in both public and private social welfare agencies and is presently an assistant professor at the School of Social Work, University of Texas at Austin, where she continues her research in the area of child support.